CURATED

—

A new experience in retail design

Nouveau design des espaces de vente

Nuevo diseño de tiendas

Nuovo design per negozi

—

promopress

CURATED

A new experience in retail design
Nouveau design des espaces de vente
Nuevo diseño de tiendas
Nuovo design per negozi

Translators of the foreword:
French / Spanish / Italian translator: Satèl.lit bcn - Olivier Gilbert / Miguel Izquierdo / Arrigo Frisano-Paulon

Copyright © 2011 by Sandu Publishing Co., Limited
Copyright © 2011 English language edition by
Promopress for sale in Europe and America.

PROMOPRESS is a commercial brand of:
Promotora de Prensa Internacional S.A.
C/ Ausiàs March, 124
08013 Barcelona, Spain
Phone: +34 93 245 14 64
Fax: +34 93 265 48 83
info@promopress.es
www.promopress.info

Cover project by Saucier + Perrotte architectes

Sponsored by: Design 360° – Concept and Design Magazine
Chief Editor: Wang Shaoqiang
Executive Editor: Eileen Punk
Chief Designer: Wang Shaoqiang
Executive Designer: Zhu Yingqi
www.sandu360.com

ISBN: 978-84-92810-25-3

Printed in China

FOREWORD

by Eileen Punk

Curated – A new experience in retail design is based on the concept that less is more, it illustrates modern interior design with extremely brief style. Projects covering a wide range of retail shops, most of which are based on an original concept that displays the products in their optimum condition. Some of the retail shops even offer food and beverage, which can make the customers understand the products better. Besides, flagship stores of famous brands like Hermès, Swarovski, Puma, and Jeanswest are role models for new minimalism. In fashion industry, they definitely have more things to demonstrate, more stories to tell than others. However, a minimalist space makes everything neat but not superficial. Then we have hair sal ons which inspire the designers most. Beauty is always affected by the surroundings. A good mood often comes from the comfortable atmosphere, which is created by a minimalist space. Showrooms are born to be in the right order. To choose a unique design language is the key to break the routines. Too much decoration may be considered to be overacting and stealing the attraction of the items. Curated also features dinning space such as cafés and pastry shops with a sense of tranquility. Giving out soft and tender lights, they are the symbolization of new minimalism interior design.

Brief style is usually considered to be pure white. Project Theurel & Thomas by Anagrama has one of the most enlightened spaces with an exclusivity and elegant atmosphere. White is their creating condition for design. Therefore, details become an essential part in such space, and it's a significant issue to build up a magnificent brand, to emphasize the unique value as well as highlight the products.

There are other ways to measure and express minimalist design despite of being completely white. White may easily go flat. Saucier + Perrotte architectes decided to play tricks with new elements in their project Boutique Michel Brisson, such as smoked glass, mirrors, and movable display elements. One of the concepts for the facade is based on the desire to reveal the modern character of the original building.

While Torafu Architects conveys minimalist design differently in the renovation project Spinning Objects by making use of installations like spinning showcase, aiming to design a strong space that could display the products effectively, and have a capacity of adding new items without changing the structure or interfering with the design. To display the products upon such circular cases creates an illusion like an after image.

Over 50 projects designed by famous designers and studios are featured in the book. All of the designers have their own understanding of minimalist design. They have unique vision of the whole fashion trend, and manage it by creating distinctive design languages and concepts. They don't have to lean on installations and decorations to dress up the shops and stores. Every single one of the ingenious elements holds a great deal of information. The less we can see from the outside, the more stories we can find.

PROLOGUE

by Eileen Punk

Curated – Nouveau design des espaces de vente est basé sur le concept du « moins est plus » (Less is more). Il illustre le design d'intérieur moderne dans à un style extrêmement épuré. Un choix complet et pertinent de projets apporte leurs réponses sur le thème des espaces de vente, dont la plupart sont basés sur un concept original qui permet de disposer les produits dans leur condition optimale. Certains de ces espaces, en cohérence avec le design, consacrent même un volume pour la restauration afin d'aider les clients à mieux comprendre les produits. Les magasins représentant les navires amiraux des grandes marques comme Hermès, Swarovski, Puma et Jeanswest sont signalés comme des modèles du nouveau minimalisme. Bien qu'ils aient certainement plus de choses à démontrer, plus d'histoires à raconter que d'autres dans l'industrie de la mode, un espace minimaliste révèle une ambiance soignée mais pas superficielle. Les salons de coiffure ont aussi leur place dans cet ouvrage car ils doivent inspirer particulièrement les designers. La beauté est toujours influencée par l'environnement. Une bonne ambiance découle souvent d'une atmosphère confortable créée par un espace minimaliste. Les espaces d'exposition naissent de l'objectif de disposer le produit à sa juste place. Choisir un langage de design singulier est la clef pour ne pas tomber dans la routine. Une décoration chargée peut être ressentie comme tape-à-l'œil et peut donc diminuer l'importance des articles d'un magasin. Curated expose également des espaces de restauration comme des cafés et des pâtisseries où règne une impression de tranquillité. En distribuant une lumière douce et harmonieuse, ils représentent le symbole de la nouvelle décoration minimaliste.

Un style épuré est généralement associé au blanc immaculé. Le projet Theurel & Thomas d'Anagrama possède des espaces lumineux et une ambiance exclusive et élégante. Le blanc est la base créative de leur design. Dans ce contexte, les détails deviennent une composante cruciale de tels espaces, et établir une marque exceptionnelle ne doit pas les sous-estimer, pour souligner son incomparable valeur et mettre en évidence ses produits.

Il y a cependant d'autres façons que l'utilisation du blanc pour traduire et exprimer un design minimaliste. Le blanc peut facilement devenir quelconque. Dans leur projet Boutique Michel Brisson, les architectes Saucier & Perrotte ont décidé de réaliser des tours de passe-passe avec de nouveaux éléments, tels que le verre fumé, les miroirs et du mobilier mobile. Le concept de la façade répond au désir de révéler le caractère moderne de l'édifice original. En revanche, Torafu Architects exprime un design minimaliste différemment dans le projet de rénovation Spinning Objects grâce à l'utilisation d'installations, comme des vitrines pivotantes, visant à concevoir un espace à caractère qui peut montrer les produits efficacement tout en préservant la possibilité d'en ajouter de nouveaux sans changer la structure ou interférer sur le design. L'exposition des produits dans ces urnes circulaires nous étonne alors avec ses effets d'optique.

Curated expose plus de 50 projets conçus par des studios et designers célèbres, chacun avec leur propre interprétation du design minimaliste. Ils ont tous une vision unique de cette tendance qui se traduit par un langage et des concepts spécifiques. Ils n'ont pas à utiliser des artifices ou des décorations superflues pour habiller les boutiques et magasins. Chacun des éléments se caractérise par son ingéniosité et inclus la juste et pertinente information. Le moins qu'on puisse voir de l'extérieur, le plus d'histoires nous seront révélées de l'intérieur.

PRÓLOGO

by Eileen Punk

Curated – Nuevo diseño de tiendas se basa en el concepto de que menos es más e ilustra el diseño de interiores moderno fundado en un estilo extremadamente esencial. Los proyectos abarcan un amplio espectro de espacios comerciales, la mayoría de los cuales se basa en el concepto original de exhibir los productos en las mejores condiciones. Algunos de estos espacios ofrecen incluso productos de alimentación, y un interiorismo que se ajuste a dicho concepto puede mejorar la identificación de sus artículos por parte de la clientela. De otra parte, aquellas tiendas que funcionan como buques insignia de marcas afamadas cuales Hermès, Swarovski, Puma y Jeanswest se constituyen en modelos a seguir en el seno del nuevo minimalismo. Pero es en la industria de la moda donde hay más cosas que demostrar y casos que contar. Un espacio minimalista genera pulcritud, pero no frivoliza necesariamente el contenido. Contamos también con los salones de peluquería, que son quizá los que más inspiran a los diseñadores. La belleza siempre se ve afectada por el entorno: una atmosfera confortable, creada a partir de un espacio minimalista, mejora a menudo el estado de ánimo. Los showrooms nacen para disponer todo en su justo orden. Optar por un lenguaje de diseño único es la clave para superar las rutinas. Al mismo tiempo, una decoración profusa puede resultar redundante y restar protagonismo a los artículos. Curated presenta también ámbitos de restauración tales como cafés y pastelerías donde impera una sensación de sosiego. Con su iluminación suave y tenue simbolizan el nuevo minimalismo en el diseño de interiores.

El estilo esencial suele asociarse a un blanco inmaculado. El proyecto Theurel & Thomas de Anagrama cuenta con uno de los espacios más avanzados por su exclusividad y elegante atmosfera. El blanco es la base creativa de sus diseños. En ese entorno, los detalles pasan a ser un factor esencial de tales espacios de cara a configurar una marca excepcional que haga hincapié en su valor único y otorgue el debido relieve a los productos.

Existen otros baremos para calibrar y expresar el diseño minimalista, más allá del color blanco, que además puede tornarse anodino. Los arquitectos Saucier & Perrotte decidieron introducir ciertos trucos mediante elementos nuevos en su proyecto de la Boutique Michel Brisson, tales como cristal ahumado, espejos y aparadores móviles. El concepto de fachada responde al deseo de revelar el carácter moderno del edificio original. A su vez, Torafu Architects aporta un diseño minimalista alternativo en la renovación del proyecto Spinning Object al recurrir a instalaciones tales como mostradores giratorios, que aspiran a conformar un espacio firme que exhiba con eficacia sus productos, y cuente con la capacidad de añadir nuevos artículos sin alterar la estructura o interferir con el diseño. La exhibición de los productos en estas urnas circulares crea una ilusión similar a la de una "postimagen".

En el libro se presentan más de 50 proyectos diseñados por profesionales y estudios renombrados. Todos ellos tienen su propia concepción del diseño minimalista y cuentan con una visión única de dicha tendencia, que gestionan mediante la creación de lenguajes y conceptos distintivos. En general, no necesitan del concurso de instalaciones o decorados para vestir tiendas y espacios comerciales. Cada uno de los ingeniosos elementos incorporados brinda una información notable. Cuanto menos veamos desde el exterior, más historias se nos van a revelar.

PREFAZIONE

by Eileen Punk

Curated – nuovo design per negozi si basa sul concetto secondo cui "poco è molto", illustrando un disegno di interni moderno con uno stile estremamente conciso. Il progetto copre un ampio spettro di negozi al dettaglio, la maggior parte dei quali basati su un concetto originale che rappresenta il prodotto nelle sue condizioni ottimali. Alcuni dei negozi al dettaglio offrono addirittura cibi e bevande che possano aiutare i clienti a comprendere meglio i prodotti. Per di più, i negozi "ammiraglia" di marche famose come Hermès, Swarovski, Puma, e Jeanswest costituiscono dei punti di riferimento e dei modelli per il nuovo minimalismo anche se nell'industria della moda avrebbero senz'altro più oggetti da esporre e storie da raccontare rispetto a tanti altri. In ogni caso, uno spazio minimalista sarà pure sgombro, ma non certo superficiale. Troviamo poi saloni di parrucchiere che rappresentano la massima fonte di ispirazione per i designer. La bellezza risente sempre dell'influenza del suo intorno. Spesso un buon umore deriva da un'atmosfera confortevole creata da uno spazio minimalista. Gli showroom esistono per disporre tutto quanto nel suo giusto ordine. La scelta di un linguaggio di design unico è la chiave per infrangere la routine. Un arredamento eccessivo può essere considerato come una mania di protagonismo, rubando la scena agli articoli.

In Curated trovano posto anche spazi per il pranzo o la cena, compresi caffè e pasticcerie con un senso di tranquillità. Offrendo luci morbide e soffuse simboleggiano il nuovo disegno di interni minimalista.

Generalmente si considera il bianco puro come il più conciso tra gli stili. Project Theurel & Thomas di Anagrama propone uno degli spazi più illuminati, con un'atmosfera esclusiva ed elegante. Il bianco è la loro condizione creativa per il design, e allora i dettagli diventano una parte essenziale in questo spazio, questione importante nella costituzione di una marca straordinaria, enfatizzandone il valore unico e mettendone in risalto i prodotti.

Esistono altri modi per valutare ed esprimere il design minimalista pure in presenza del bianco totale. Il bianco può diventare facilmente noioso. Saucier + Perrotte Architects hanno deciso di giocherellare con nuovi elementi nel loro progetto Boutique Michel Brisson, con vetri fumé, specchi ed elementi espositivi mobili. Uno dei concept per la facciata si basa sul desiderio di svelare il carattere moderno dell'edificio originale.

Da parte loro, Torafu Architects trasmettono il design minimalista in modo diverso nel progetto di ristrutturazione Spinning Objects, sfruttando installazioni come vetrine girevoli e puntando a disegnare uno spazio forte in grado di presentare efficacemente i prodotti, con facoltà di aggiungere nuovi elementi senza alterare la struttura o interferire con il design. La presentazione dei prodotti in questi involucri circolari crea un'illusione simile a un'immagine persistente.

Il libro propone oltre 50 progetti creati da designer famosi, ciascuno dei quali con il proprio personale approccio al disegno minimalista, con la propria visione individuale e unica del complesso delle tendenze della moda, affrontate creando linguaggi di design e concept caratteristici. Non devono per forza appoggiarsi a installazioni o decorazioni per vestire negozi e botteghe. Ogni singolo ingegnoso elemento racchiude in sé informazioni in abbondanza. Meno possiamo vedere dall'esterno, più storie sapremo trovare.

CONTENTS

Salon du Fromage
kotaro horiuchi architecture

Design: Kotaro Horiuchi Architecture
Client: Salon du Fromage
Photography: Koichi HIROSE and Hiroki TAGMA
Site: Paris, France
Area: 73 sqm
Restaurant

On the ground floor and the first floor, a wall with curved surfaces was designed to wrap around the space softly. The existing building was built in the 18th century.

Pierce the wall of the building and selling as well as eating cheese in it integrally changed the space like cheese with caves.

In the narrow space of the ground floor, refrigerated displays units with different diameter and heights cylindrical since there are 350 kinds of cheeses for customers to appreciate in this space.

Customers select and taste cheese and also find their favorite savor there.

Pass through a wall with curved surfaces, there is a restaurant up stairs.

The space is furnished with tables and chairs, also a remaining place for an open kitchen. Customers can select wines while enjoying their cheese fondues.

The restaurant with an open kitchen has been design to host various events such as cheese seminars, wine classes or cooking classes.

In the cheese ripening space, it also can turn into a cooking preparation space or a lounge for employees, even an expansion space for cooking class.

T-magi
WE Architecture

Design: WE Architecture
Client: T-magi
Photography: Enok Holsegaard
Site: Copenhagen, Denmark
Area: 60 sqm
Retail store

While a lot of shops tend to have a clear distinction between storefront and interior, the design of T-magi allows the shop itself to be perceived as the display window. WE has used the teapot, an object universally associated with tea, as the motif of the shop, also its logo and PR material. They've intentionally designed the shop with a feeling of Lab, inviting people to pass by, smell 40 different kinds of teas displayed on the scent wall. Have a taste, read the WE-tea folder or simply browse the exclusive products of Marriage frère sold in the shop. Tiny backlit holes perforate the shelves and back wall providing a large 3-dimensional image of a Teapot, such a powerful eye-catcher. The image of the Teapot dissolves when you approach, and it becomes a furnishing of the shop.

Theurel & Thomas
Anagrama

Design: *Anagrama*
Client: *Theurel & Thomas*
Photography: *Carlos Rodríguez*
Site: *San Pedro, Mexico*
Area: *40 sqm*
Retail store

Theurel & Thomas is the first pastry store in Mexico specialized in French macarons, the most popular dessert of the French pastries.

One of the most important extensions of a brand, which has a business based in store selling, is the design and ambiance of the stores.

For this project, it was very important to create an imposing brand that would emphasize the unique value, elegance and detail of this delicate dessert.

The Theurel & Thomas pâtisserie has an enlightened space with an exclusivity and elegant atmosphere. The store location is in San Pedro, Mexico, Latin America's most affluent suburb.

White was their primary tool for design. As a result of this the attention was fully oriented to the colorful macarons. They placed two lines in their design in cyan and magenta, as a relation with a modern French flag to inject a vanguard vision to the identity. They selected Didot (a French typography created by Firmin and Pierre Didot) to present the brand with sophistication.

Details were an essential part of their work. The designers meticulously selected each porcelain piece creating a balance with sophisticated specks, which improves the value of the brand and outshine the product.

koichiro kimura
aoyama
art·craft international

Design: koichiro kimura
Client: koichiro kimura aoyama
Photography: nobuo yano, koichiro kimura
Site: Tokyo, Japan
Area: 30 sqm
Retail store

The shop koichiro kimura aoyama opened in Tokyo. Art·craft international wanted to realize its artistic sensibility in a concrete way and present to the world's avant garde field that it has a unique way of breaking through into the world. Furthermore, the designers hoped that the opening of the Tokyo store would provide greater opportunity to connect new and diverse groups of people.

The first floor is a shop and the second floor is a gallery space. The designer can spend his time hiding behind the pink wall. When customers walk into the shop, he can appear like a ninja.

The second floor is created with the motif of a holy woman's room inside a pyramid. The designer feels that, for a holy woman's room, making out of pyramids can create greater "pyramid power". And it seems that as if a god of creative power could come down and alight here.

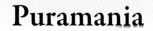

Puramania
Studio Guilherme Torres

Design: *Guilherme Torres*
Client: *Puramania*
Photography: *Denilson Machado – MCA Estúdio*
Site: *São Paulo, Brazil*
Area: *354 sqm*
Retail store

The format of the terrain, which was completely irregular with a 1.8m acclivity going from the street level to the back of the lot, in addition to a no wider than 2.8m narrowing point, made this place an almost impracticable one. However, after a year of extensive renovation, the lot was ready to host a young fashion brand store. The main fundamentals of the project was precisely to fall back on the narrowest point of the building to act as the core of the store, which therefore, escapes from the common place projects usually associated with brands of jeans. The project inspires a futuristic atmosphere where several cubes arise on and off, sometimes hanging from the ceiling, other times emerging from the floor, giving shape to counters, niches and showcases. All the structures in the building were made of metal structures, coated with drywalls and painted with epoxy. The lighting is composed of a mix between glass domes, designed to capture the most sunlight, and huge panels of polyurethane tensioned screens that eradiate dim fluorescent light. The energy efficiency and a low rate of waste, added to logic in the use of appropriate materials brought about an ideal atmosphere to create a symbol for the brand, which has recently become part of the fashion scenario in São Paulo.

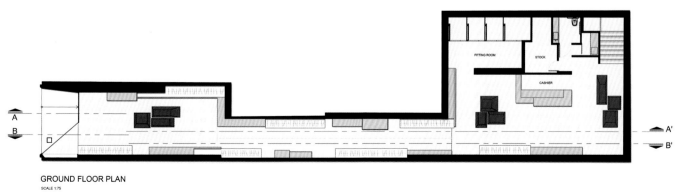

GROUND FLOOR PLAN

SCALE 1:75

0 1 2 3   5   10

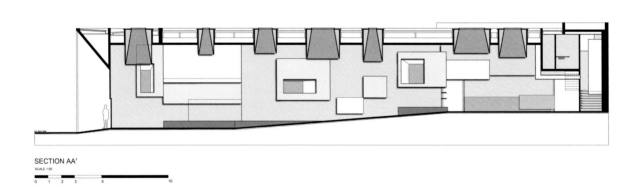

SECTION AA'

SCALE 1:50

0 1 2 3   5   10

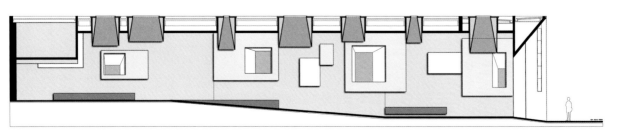

SECTION BB'

SCALE 1:50

0 1 2 3   5   10

Cristiano Cora
Avi Oster Studio

Design: Avi Oster
Client: Cristiano Cora
Photography: Mikiko Kikuyama
Site: New York, USA
Area: 2000 sf
Salon

The vision for this project evolved gradually. Avi Oster's aim was to create a space that would be distinctly appealing to women, something slightly curved, clean, and stylish, at the same time, comforting and transformational. Avi Oster began to think about the concept of a shell or cave, even some extremely basic protective and comforting form that folds around a being, and this motif found its way into the design of the space.

The designers tried to keep everything clean and to eliminate more information or distraction besides the experience of the client and the stylist. For instance, there is a separate wet and dry room for laundry services which is kept discreet by a hidden door. They also designed the floor to curve upwards to enable easy sweeping of the hair to the vacuum system's nozzles at the edge of the floor.

One of the client's experiences is transformation. At Cristiano, the simplicity of the design encourages the client's focus to be on the inspiring experience of becoming transformed. In this salon, the designers wanted to create the sensation for a woman to enter a protected space and emerge transformed, purified, indulged, comforted, and relaxed.

The most unique material the designers used in this project was the Newmat Light Stretch Ceiling. Developed in France and made from latex, it provides a stretch ceiling that customers can use to cover large spaces and create a kind of skin.

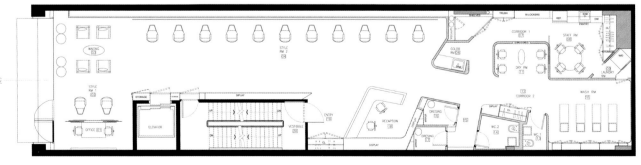

1 CRISTIANO CORA PLAN
1/4"=1'-0"   N

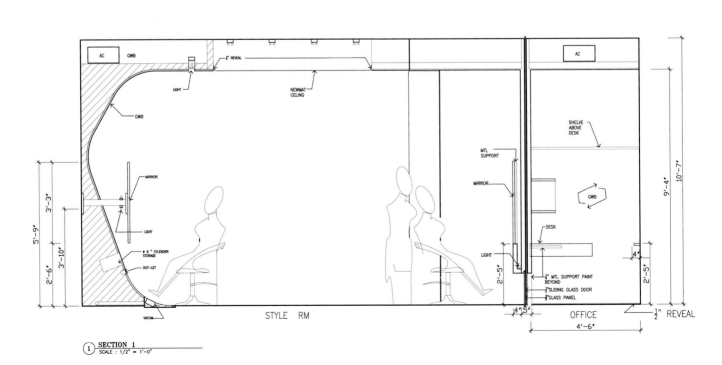

AC	GWB	½" REVEAL				AC

LIGHT

NEWMAT
CELING

GWB

SHELVE
ABOVE
DESK

MTL
SUPPORT

MIRROR

MIRROR

GWB

DESK

LIGHT

LIGHT

6 " CYLENDER
STORAGE

OUT-LET

1" MTL SUPPORT PAINT
BEYOND

½" SLIDING GLASS DOOR

¼"GLASS PANEL

VACUM

5'-9"

3'-3"

3'-10"

2'-6"

2'-5"

STYLE   RM

4"5'

4'-6"

OFFICE

2'-5"

4"

½ " REVEAL

9'-4"

10'-7"

Marco & Mari in Beijing

SAKO Architects

Design: *Keiichiro SAKO, Toru IWASA, Nobutoshi HARA / SAKO Architects*
Client: *Marco & Mari (Shanghai) Company Limited*
Photography: *Misae Hiromatsu*
Site: *Beijing, China*
Area: *89 sqm*
Retail store

"Marco & Mari in Beijing" is a children's clothing boutique, which was designed as the first renewal shop of the brand. Based on the theme of the brand, the design was expected to use European elements.

To respond the brand theme, SAKO Architects used arch, which is one of the most standardized structure form, classic European architecture, and reform the contemporary decoration. The new decorative arch is a rounded design like marshmallow or children's clay work.

Fine texture of the plaster covers the surface of the arch, giving viewers the impression of the soft cotton candy. The space is created by combining and contrasting expression, the dynamism of arches and cuteness of children's clothes.

This arch has continuously expanded to four sides around the store, which followed the classical architectural symmetry configuration. In the center surrounded by such a continuous arch, there is a cozy space where parents and children can rest together, and it will remind Foley standing in the courtyard.

This resting place and furniture also has been used to repetitive arches and marshmallow-decoration, which pulled the whole look together.

The Gourmet Tea
ALAN CHU

Design: *Alan Chu*
Client: *The Gourmet Tea*
Photography: *Djan Chu*
Site: *São Paulo, Brazil*
Area: *90 sqm*
Retail store

The colors of the little tins of the 35 blends offered by The Gourmet Tea are the inspiration for the first teahouse of this brand.

The design aims an economic solution to rapidly transform the small house into a concept store.

The walls were peeled, the structure and the bricks which became apparent were painted with white color, the original floor was maintained, the roof was lowered in order to eliminate interference of the beams and allow the indirect and continuous lightning which sweeps the walls emphasizing the depth of the long and narrow space of the building.

The only furniture made of plywood on which a colorful adhesive was applied, organizes all the space of the shop. It gathers balcony, store, box, tidbits and staging area.

The minimalist organization of the space associated with the simplicity of finishes allows the product (tea) stands out in a precise and smooth way.

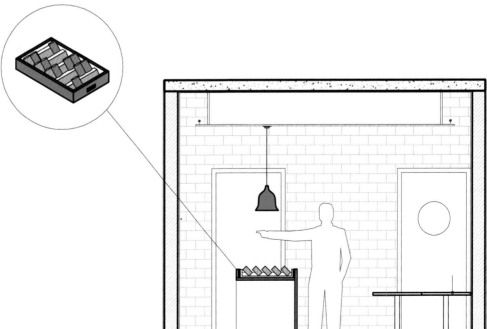

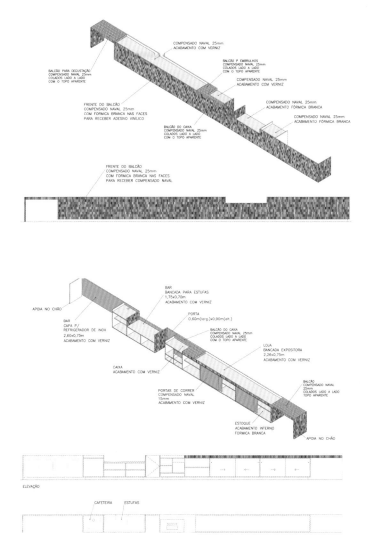

BALCÃO PARA DEGUSTAÇÃO
COMPENSADO NAVAL 25mm
COLADOS LADO A LADO
COM O TOPO APARENTE

COMPENSADO NAVAL 25mm
ACABAMENTO COM VERNIZ

BALCÃO P EMBRULHOS
COMPENSADO NAVAL 25mm
COLADOS LADO A LADO
COM O TOPO APARENTE

FRENTE DO BALCÃO
COMPENSADO NAVAL 25mm
COM FÓRMICA BRANCA NAS FACES
PARA RECEBER ADESIVO VINÍLICO

COMPENSADO NAVAL 25mm
ACABAMENTO COM VERNIZ

BALCÃO DO CAIXA
COMPENSADO NAVAL 25mm
COLADOS LADO A LADO
COM O TOPO APARENTE

COMPENSADO NAVAL 25mm
ACABAMENTO FÓRMICA BRANCA

COMPENSADO NAVAL 25mm
ACABAMENTO FÓRMICA BRANCA

FRENTE DO BALCÃO
COMPENSADO NAVAL 25mm
COM FÓRMICA BRANCA NAS FACES
PARA RECEBER COMPENSADO NAVAL

APOIA NO CHÃO

BAR
CAPA P/
REFRIGERADOR DE INOX
2,60x0,75m
ACABAMENTO COM VERNIZ

BAR
BANCADA PARA ESTUFAS
1,75x0,70m
ACABAMENTO COM VERNIZ

PORTA
0,60m(larg.)x0,90m(alt.)

BALCÃO DO CAIXA
COMPENSADO NAVAL 25mm
COLADOS LADO A LADO
COM O TOPO APARENTE

LOJA
BANCADA EXPOSITORA
2,26x0,75m
ACABAMENTO COM VERNIZ

CAIXA
ACABAMENTO COM VERNIZ

PORTAS DE CORRER
COMPENSADO NAVAL
15mm
ACABAMENTO COM VERNIZ

BALCÃO
COMPENSADO NAVAL
25mm
COLADOS LADO A LADO
TOPO APARENTE

ESTOQUE
ACABAMENTO INTERNO
FÓRMICA BRANCA

APOIA NO CHÃO

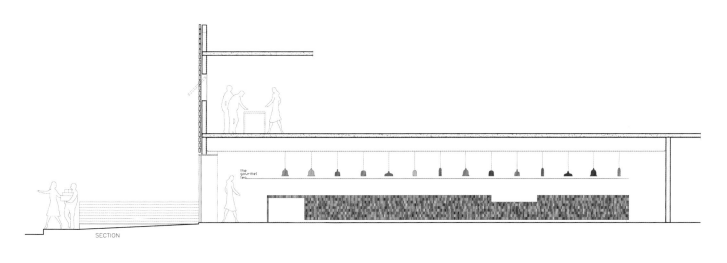

ELEVAÇÃO

CAFETEIRA   ESTUFAS

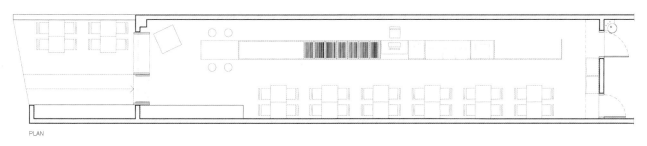

SECTION

the gourmet tea

PLAN

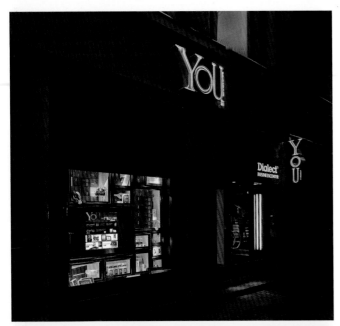

You by Dialect
Electric Dreams AB

Design: C. Frankander, J. Degermark, S. Otley
Client: You by Dialect
Photography: Cesar af Reis
Site: Stockholm, Sweden
Area: 120 sqm
Retail store

The You by Dialect store in central Stockholm features a friendly and playful environment. It's more reminiscent of somebody's quirky living room than traditional all-white consumer electronics interiors. The store invites customers to relax, drink a cup of coffee and really try out the products before buying. The product range is a mix of the latest gadgets and the best accessories to go with them.

The product displays are a collection of different glossy black picture frames of different dimensions, hiding in-store communication screens and integrated lighting. The giant purple lamp shades were upholstered with double-sided silk fabric on steel wireframes. The chandelier is made from thousands of lacquered mirror Perspex logotypes, individually hung on fishing line from perforated metal panels.

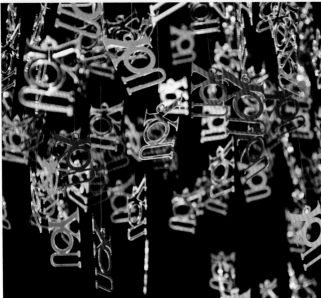

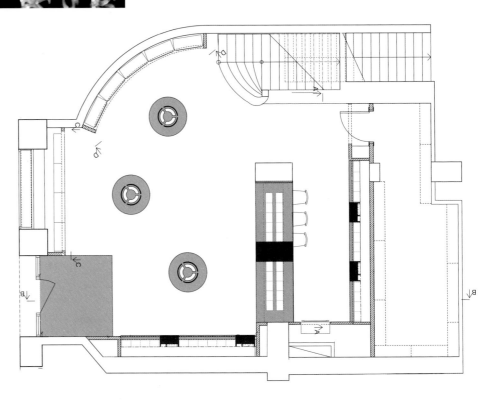

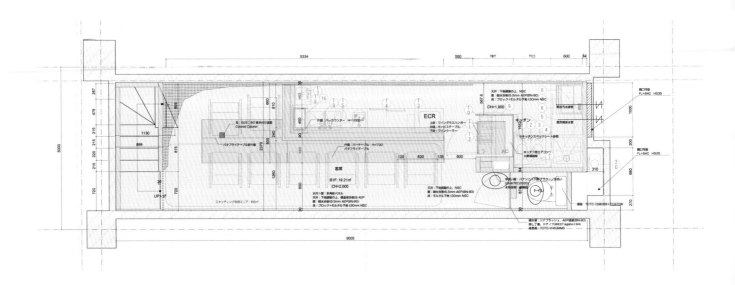

Lucien Pellat-Finet Shinsaibashi

Kengo Kuma & Associates

Design: *Kengo Kuma & Associates*
Client: *Coronet Corporation*
Photography: *Daici Ano*
Site: *Osaka, Japan*
Area: *133 sqm*
Retail store

In the meeting at Shinsaibashi, looking down the street of luxurious brand shops, Lucien asked for a soft and warm space rather than an icy and solid one. In response to his idea, the designer proposed a plan to realize the softness of Lucien Pellar-Finet cashmere in the architecture. In seeking balance between the cost and the creation of various organic patterns, a "vegetable wall" was born, which is made of structural plywood with two kinds of width and three types of aluminum connectors. From just beside, it looks that pentagons and parallelogram are repeated and extended further in the interior like a cave, creating a honeycomb-like internal space with lots of different cells. By changing the cutting of sections, each cell in the wall has become practical fittings, like a shelf or box to place the products. Rather than setting in an individual wall or furniture separately in the shop, the designer wanted to create a single, sequenced and functional wall which can cover the entire space. This vegetable wall grows like a liana, from the café in the basement towards the boutique on the first and the second floor and the library on the top floor, and among the "vines" come out cashmeres like fruits born from the plant. It was collaboration between fashion and plant-likened architecture.

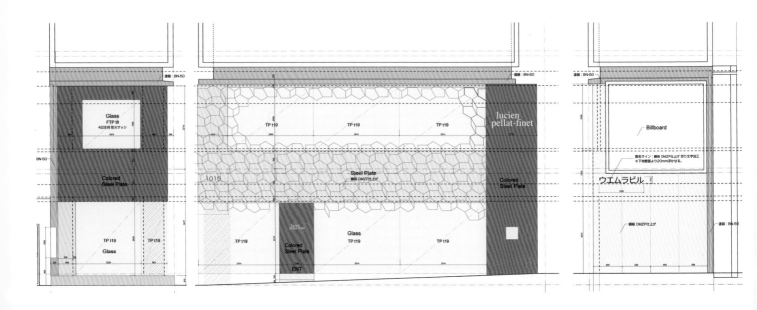

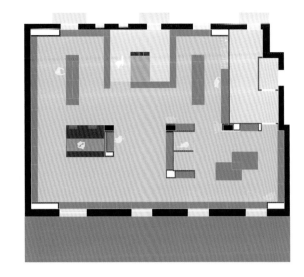

Muji shop in Milano
Roberto Murgia Architetto, Studio Fase, Aliverti Samsa Architetti

Design: Roberto Murgia Architetto, Studio Fase, Aliverti Samsa Architetti
Client: Muji italia spa
Photography: Giovanna Silva
Site: Milan, Italy
Area: 300 sqm
Retail store

Every new Muji store is essential. It is made for displaying the products. It reflects the brand's packaging that is reduced to the minimum. A showcase without showing off. A new project for each city but all linked together. Different outlets related to a single philosophy.

The philosophy of simplification is: to reduce any unnecessary gesture, decoration and excess. The Milan store is on two levels, a small room at street level and the rest at the first floor. On the ground floor, in a long and narrow space, glass shelves are used to accommodate merchandise. Same finish for the treads of the staircase Muji's brief was essential in line with its philosophy. Light colors, natural materials and matte surfaces. White is used throughout, with some stainless steel and timber exceptions. Light fittings are fixed on a custom perforated white painted steel channel which follows the arrangement of the furniture.

Flatform 322
Toby Horrocks Architecture and Autumn Products

Design: *Toby Horrocks and Kristian Aus*
Client: *Design Dispensary*
Photography: *Ellen Dewar*
Site: *Victoria, Australia*
Area: *20 sqm*
Retail store

Interiors and products have a limited life span. Do you design for longevity and hope your designs don't prematurely end up in the garbage bin? Or go with the flow and accept that change is inevitable? Designed for the Look, Shop exhibition of Melbourne shop windows during the Victorian State of Design Festival, industrial designer Kristian Aus and architect Toby Horrocks created an interior space that is both architecture and object. An experiment with a playful idea, the project is also principled in its consideration of material life-cycle. Cardboard is a material made from post-consumer waste, and one that is easily recycled. The project is partly a critique of contemporary retail fitouts that "churn" on a regular basis, and partly an antidote.

A pop-up booked crossed with a serious retail display system, folding wall panels move between 2D and 3D states. Flat panels fold down to create functional shelving, a table, lamp shades and a seat. Panels are joined using wing nuts, which are painted green and exposed – no glue is used – the entire thing is demountable and flat-packed. The wall panels are offset from the walls of the existing retail space, and the voids created by the fold-down furniture expose glimpses of the existing fittings.

The decision to use cardboard impacted positively on the project budget, as cardboard is a low-cost material. Even when allowing for the digital creation process, the project's design and formation was extremely cost effective. The structures are also designed for multiple uses, so therefore once cut it can be used again and again in additional installations at no added cost. This project develops a model for a sustainable, temporary interior, that is both playful and principled.

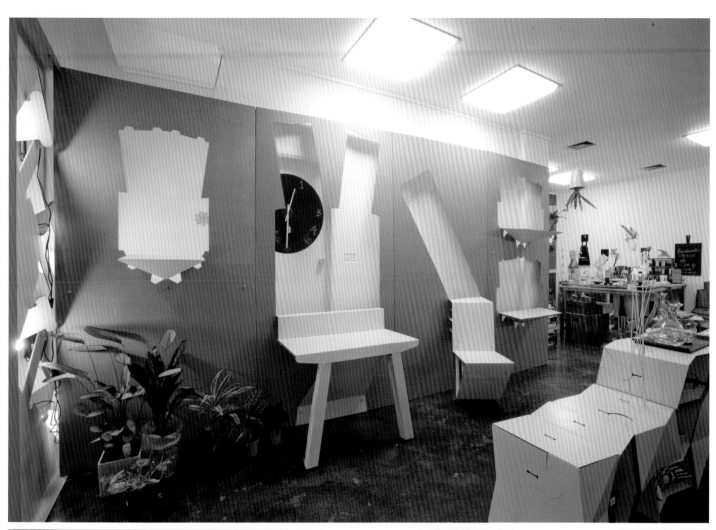

JEANSWEST
in Wuxi

SAKO Architects

Design: *Keiichiro SAKO, Tomoaki MURATA / SAKO Architects*
Client: *JeansWest international(HK)LTD.*
Photography: *Zhonghai SHEN*
Site: *Wuxi, China*
Area: *360 sqm*
Retail store

The logistics plays an important role in the modern life of consumption. And the wooden crate can be seen as the symbol of logistics. It is interesting that the wooden crate can be used to create the space which can stimulate customers' desire to consume, which is the purpose of creation. Let's imagine that there are 150 wooden crates in the white room of 300 square meters, some are connective with each other, and some are separated, which make up a three-dimensional space.

The decoration inside the store will direct the customers to discover the interest of shopping. Different from other retail stores, customers feel like enter the storehouse where others are unloading the goods, which excites them by choosing the product that they really want from thousands of goods.

MON LOU LOU

assistant Co., Ltd.

Design: *Megumi Matsubara, Hiroi Ariyama*
Client: *Mon Lou Lou*
Photography: *Motohiro Sunouchi*
Site: *Tokyo, Japan*
Area: *61.5 sqm*
Salon

The hair salon is located on a small local shopping street at the ground level of a narrow building with entrances on both ends. The interior design concept derived from joy and adventure of finding a small hidden street which connects with two places. It consists of moving wall panels that function as doors to staff rooms and coat racks and so on. When the panels move, bright colors of painted walls on the other side of the simple wall surfaces show up.

The salon is enlightened by people's movement. The dual nature of the walls accentuates the joy of discovering new space, walking in and out.

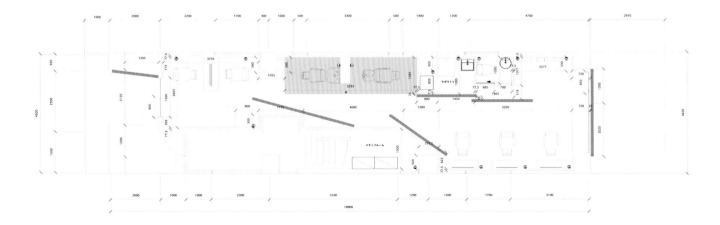

Aesop Pop-Up
March Studio

March Studio's 8th project for Australian cosmetic brand Aesop is a pop-up store at Paris based department store Merci. March Studio was inspired to create an organic, flowing space to mark Aesop's arrival at Merci. Consisting of 4500 cardboard shipper boxes (the very same boxes that Aesop uses to ship their product worldwide), the boxes were trapped in a 40 sqm net to form a continuous wall and ceiling feature.

The project is emblematic of March Studio's play on repetition and the elevation of everyday objects from commonplace to statement. The project is inherently resourceful and sustainable in that the boxes will be reused after the deinstall and shipped out to customers through Aesop's mail order system.

Design: *March Studio*
Client: *Aesop*
Photography: *Louis Baquiast*
Site: *Paris, France*
Area: *40 sqm*
Retail store

Aesop Singapore
March Studio

Design: *March Studio*
Client: *Aesop*
Photography: *Edward Hendricks*
Site: *Singapore*
Retail store

Singapore continues the March Studio - Aesop dialogue of contextualization and materiality. From cardboard boxes to amber glass bottles, Swiss hoarding boards to white porcelain. Each exploration is an exercise of opportunity and constraint of a local material.

The (new) Singapore store offered a unique challenge to a city truly searching for an identity away from the glistening shopping malls and bright neon lights.

Throughout history Singapore is a trade route, a midway point, or a half way stops to Europe that is for the Australians. The history of transitional movement evoked the designers' ideas of lineage and passage making, of the many journeys taken into, and then out of the wonderful city.

String was first sought as a representation of the diagram, a diagram with lines converging to one point not too dissimilar to the one on the inside jacket of the in-flight manual.

Thirty kilometers of coconut husk String, a regional product, is employed to create a dynamic light fixture and chandelier. The seemingly insignificant threads when combined on mass mesmerize.

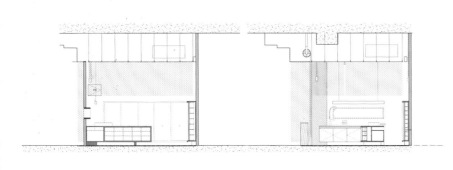

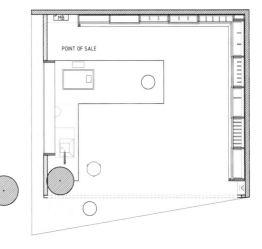

POINT OF SALE

01 SECTION X
AESOP - SINGAPORE

02 SECTION Y
AESOP - SINGAPORE

CARHARTT
FRANCES RIFE STUDIO

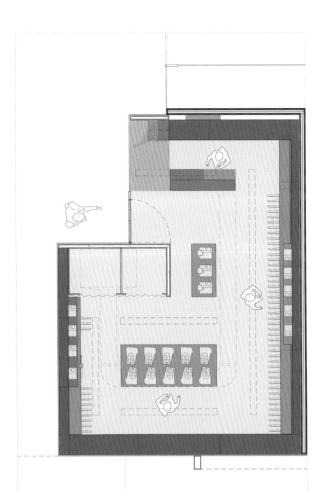

Design: FRANCES RIFE
Client: CARHARTT
Photography: FERNANDO ACDA
Site: Barcelona, Spain
Area: 43 sqm
Retail store

The new concept stores Carhartt intended to reflect the philosophy of a brand, which was born for American workers to dress the old west. Until now, it has always remained true to its origins: making good quality clothes, comfortable and as durable as possible. In this case, it becomes increasingly difficult to find companies that have not altered or changed their product line with current trends. The timelessness, the genuine commitment, and the raw material itself contribute to the sustainability of a brand. Therefore, this is what required for a project.

Under that premise, the designers presented the project inspired by the natural recovery of the raw material itself, and thus was chosen as the main material for wrapping the store, untreated solid wood, creating a structure based on stacked ribbons, as stored in the old mills, they are the source of the material which transformed by then.

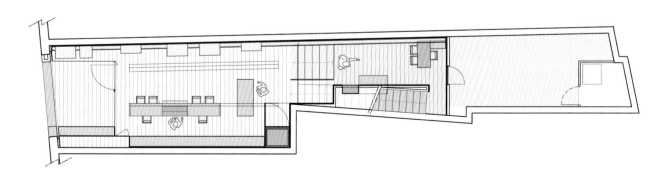

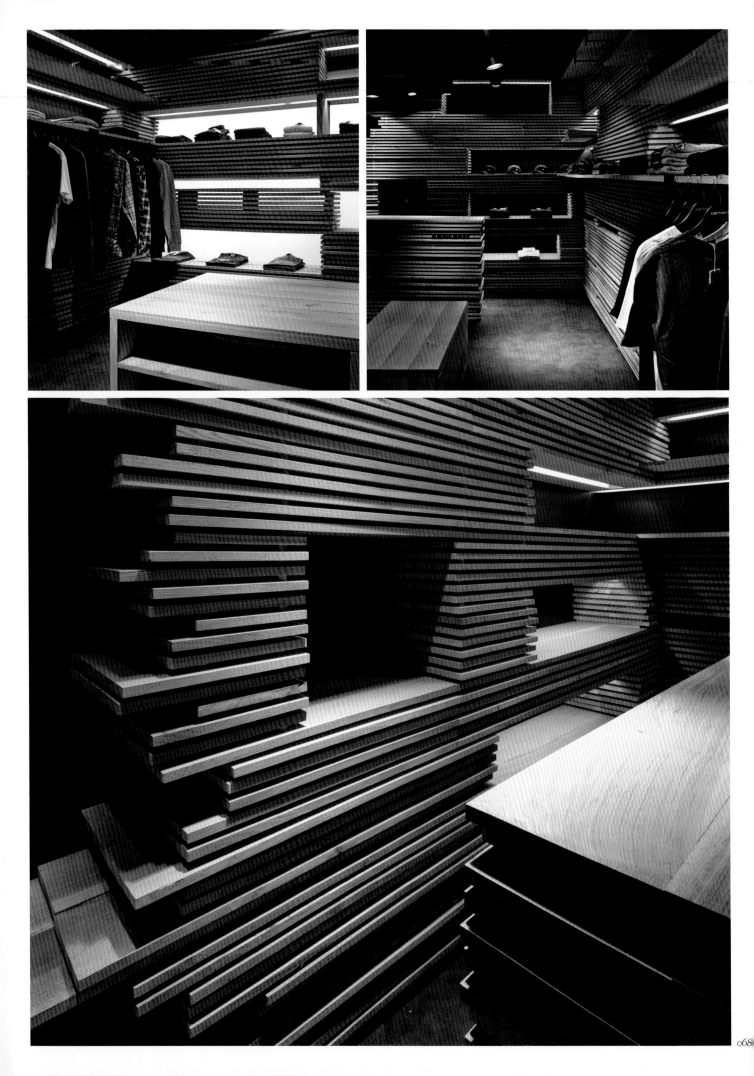

Hairstyling Nafi, Basel

ZMIK in collaboration with SÜDQUAI patente. unikate.

Design: *ZMIK in collaboration with SÜDQUAI patente.unikate.*
Client: *Hairstyling Nafi, Basel*
Photography: *Eik Frenzel*
Site: *Basel, Switzerland*
Area: *100 sqm*
Salon

The hairdresser Hairstyling Nafi in Basel's historic city centre has undergone a reconstruction. The space is now subdivided into two zones, which are being separated by a sharp border. The two areas strongly contrast in their function as well as in their spatial atmosphere. The ceiling and the walls of the reception zone are entirely covered with vintage cuttings from Vogue, photocopied onto packaging paper. Opulently furnished and bathed in warm light, the reception is an invitation for a rest, for purchasing products and for discussing the newest styling – trends. The white studio, however, is the absolute antithesis. Here nothing distracts the work of the hair stylist. The ideal light for working, the bright and glossy surfaces and the minimal, metallic furnishings put the newly cut hairstyles into the centre of attention. The customer – literally being framed by the mirror – brings the room alive with the reflection of his face.

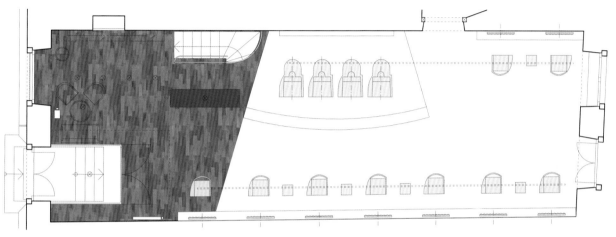

JOYERIA D
VAÍLLO & IRIGARAY + GALAR

Design: VAÍLLO & IRIGARAY + GALAR
Client: Danieli Joyeros
Photography: Jose M. Cutillas
Site: Pamplona, Spain
Area: 30 sqm
Retail store

The project intends to create an atmosphere. And, therefore, a universe (not a shop) in these little premises of 30 square meters in the city center, whose rectangular, deep and narrow geometry has to contain the elements of jewelry. The project accounts for a small black hole within the urban magma. The project again, takes up the archaic magical conception that surrounds the universe of the jewel, valuable, unique, and the odd.

It proposes against the usual crowded shops filled with jewelry. The wrapped and valuable pieces are displayed, as unique, exclusive to achieve this. An atmosphere is created, which is mysterious, strange, hollow, weightless, also Oriental and Baroque. It is originated through a geometry that encloses like a chest or a jewellery box, being able to house the content with the delicacy and mystery of valuable, unique piece of demands. The access to this space and the search for the valuable object is intended to become a magical and attractive tour. Once you trespass the mysterious jeweler's threshold, you are no longer just shopping for jewels. On one hand, the access to a solemn act is the rite of seeking an unknown small hidden treasure. On the other hand, to cross the line that leads to the mysterious and magical.

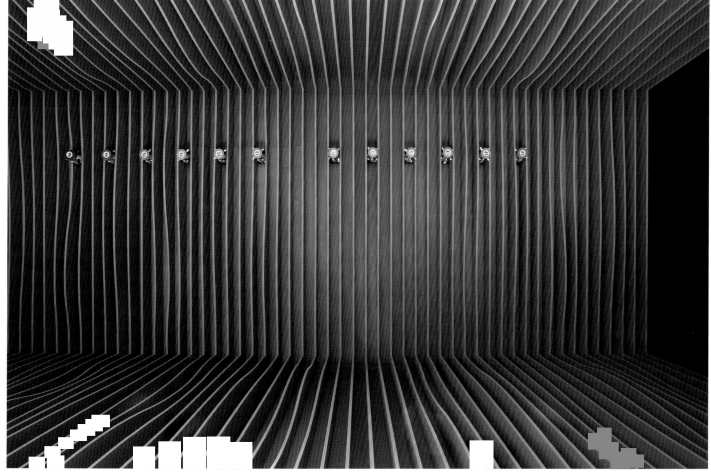

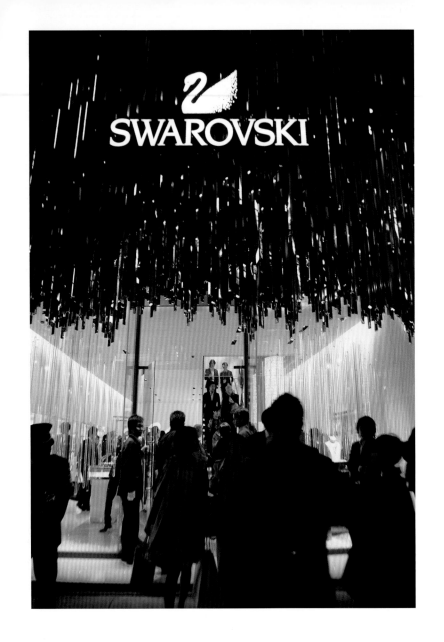

SWAROVSKI GINZA
Tokujin Yoshioka

Design: Tokujin Yoshioka
Client: Swarovski
Site: Tokyo, Japan
Area: 184.55 sqm
Retail store

This is a large project implemented by Swarovski to renew boutiques and concessions in all major fashion capitals around the world.

It was the year 2005 when Tokujin Yoshioka first worked with Swarovski for the project called Swarovski Crystal Palace. For this landmark project, in which Swarovski invites designers from around the world to create chandeliers, Tokujin Yoshioka designed a futuristic chandelier entitled "STARDUST" which projects images on each crystal component through the use of fiber optic. This design visualized a scene, which he saw in a dream on one night, that the sky is studded with countless transparent particles of light as if this fantastic sight were floating in the air.

In 2006, Swarovski appointed architects and designers for the design competition for the new store design concept and Tokujin Yoshioka was fortunate to be nominated as a designer to create and develop a new Swarovski retail concept.

The new store in Ginza is completed as the first flagship ever Swarovski showcases in the world. The concept of the new retail architecture, "Crystal Forest", is comprehensively implemented in this store design.

DJS
PANORAMA

Design: PANORAMA
Client: China Resources Retail (Corp.) Ltd.
Photography: NG SIU FUNG
Site: Hong Kong, China
Area: 100 sqm
Retail store

DJS is a new jewellery label launched by Chinese Arts & Crafts (HK) Ltd. selling diamond & jade. It is a total branding exercise to offer new retail experience of a jewellery store targeted at middle class customer group in the local competitive market.

The interior & C.I. design strategy adopted was to make use of the common natures / chemical structures & cut shape "facets" of diamond & jade to generate a unique identity for the brand.

To achieve this, the interior design made use of the metaphor of interpreting the retail space as a glowing gemstone to contain the two different types of prestigious merchandises for the customer to explore.

White spatial envelope of glowing alabaster showcase wall units and white marble floor were firstly set up to provide a minimal setting to the space. Symmetrical layout was then adopted to echo the squareness of the site. This was followed by combining the geometrical composition of facets in both aesthetic & functional layers.

White glowing wall units with tilted vertical faces in random angles allow green side facings to be exposed. This subtle addition of accent green depicts the natural beauty of jade's color and translucency. Rows of floating glazed "showcase squares" with different sizes and heights created rhythm and strong visual attractions for the customers. Small & precious items of diamond & jade displayed on custom-made frosted acrylic display stands were front & back-lit within each showcase and sculptural island unit to give sparkling & translucent beauty respectively.

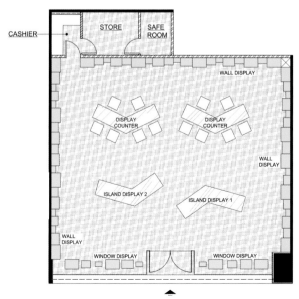

LAYOUT PLAN

CASHIER

STORE SAFE ROOM

WALL DISPLAY

DISPLAY COUNTER   DISPLAY COUNTER

WALL DISPLAY

ISLAND DISPLAY 2   ISLAND DISPLAY 1

WALL DISPLAY

WINDOW DISPLAY   WINDOW DISPLAY

REFLECTED CEILING PLAN

CASHIER STORE SAFE ROOM

CASHIER

Air slot

Air slot   Air slot

ST/ST W/. MIRROR FIN.

Air slot

+2100

International KOGEI Triennale
Nendo

Design: *Nendo*
Client: *Kanazawa City*
Photography: *Daici Ano*
Site: *Kanazawa, Japan*
Area: *1200 sqm*
Showroom

The venue called Rifare was formly a remaining space left over from a large bookstore, and its temporary use as an exhibition venue necessitated the empty retail space be left more or less intact, without placing drastic changes to the leftover interior. Working within a limited budget, Nendo was also required to obtain ample space which was used by five curators.

For this reason, Nendo decided that they would set up five pre-fabricated agricultural greenhouses made of plastic within the venue space, and turn them into individual gallery spaces. The lighting used to highlight the works inside would softly pour from the translucent plastic walls, and their gentle glow turned the greenhouses into large lanterns of light. Moreover, winding "trails" of black stapled carpets ran throughout the exhibition venue, with white vinyl panels for displaying the works positioned alongside the "trails".

While keeping costs low, the designer was able to create the semblance of "farmland" that partitioned the area where people would walk and where the works would be displayed. This form of expression was actually an expanded version of the "home-use greenhouse" that the designers had used at their pre-event venue held half a year earlier, and they found that this environment was most suitable for expressing the development and growth of crafts in the unique "soils" of Kanazawa.

Boutique Michel Brisson

Saucier + Perrotte architectes

Design: *Gilles Saucier, Charles-Alexandre Dubois*
Client: *Michel Brisson*
Photography: *Marc Cramer, Gilles Saucier*
Site: *Montreal, Canada*
Area: *411 sqm*
Retail store

To transform this seventies era, modern heritage building (formerly a National Bank), into a new space dedicated to contemporary fashion, the first step taken by the architects was to simplify the overall structure, which had been subjected over the years to a series of additions and renovations. The building's interior was thus stripped to its original brutalist structure, which revealed itself to be surprisingly striking. The sculpted, corrugated concrete of the vault and mezzanine, the structural supports, and the original exterior brick together became the mineral shell from which the project took shape.

The ensemble of the new elements, such as smoked glass, mirrors, and movable display elements (of painted aluminum and rubber) work in counterpoint to the building's original structure. The luminous ceiling stretches to fit the form of the mezzanine. The ceiling, therefore, illuminates the zone of the movable display cases, and contrasts with the clothing racks, which function as linear lighting for the space, suspended from the second floor ceiling like stalactites. The original curving staircase dramatizes the moment one reaches the second floor, where the designers found Michel Brisson's office and the V.I.P. room. Various service spaces are also located on the second floor, toward the south portion of the building.

The concept for the facade of the Michel Brisson Boutique is based not only on the desire to reveal the modern character of the original building, but also on preserving the urban continuity of Laurier Street West, which is comprised of upscale boutiques, salons, and restaurants.

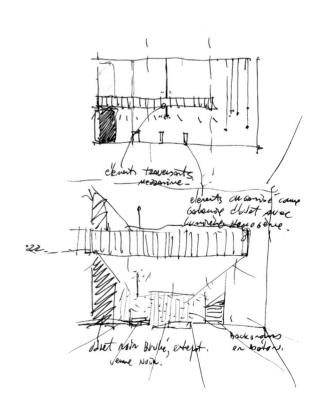

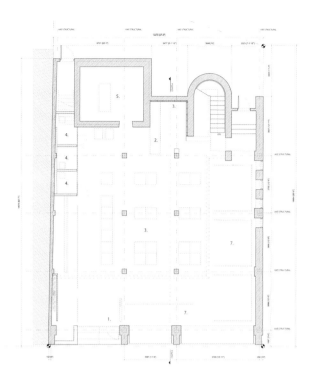

PLAN LEVEL 1 (RDC)

1. ENTRANCE
2. COUNTER
3. DISPLAY CASES
4. FITTING ROOMS
5. STORAGE SPACE
6. VIP SPACE
7. SUSPENDED RACKING

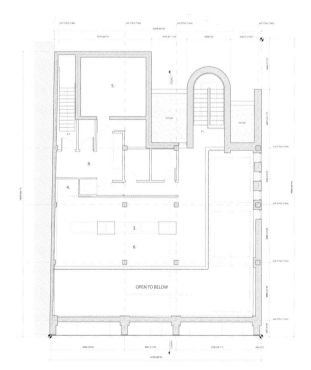

PLAN MEZZANINE

1. ENTRANCE
2. COUNTER
3. DISPLAY CASES
4. FITTING ROOMS
5. STORAGE SPACE
6. VIP SPACE
7. SUSPENDED RACKING
8. KITCHEN

Boutique Dubuc
Quebec
Saucier + Perrotte
architectes

Design: Gilles Saucier, Charles-Alexandre Dubois
Client: Philippe Dubuc
Photography: Jean Longpré
Site: Quebec, Canada
Area: 130 sqm
Retail store

Located on St-Joseph Street facing the Church of St-Roch, the new Philippe Dubuc store marks the arrival of the renowned fashion label to old Quebec City. The boutique is housed in a simple, linear space at the ground level of an existing historic building. The space itself is intersected by a large steel truss that recalls the massive structural elements from industrial times in Quebec. The design concept plays with a shift in perception between the actual dimensions of the boutique and those of a virtual space perceived by clients and visitors a "space" relating to both the larger structure of the building and to the peculiar mirrored quality of the interior.

At first glance, visitors will notice a strip of black at the left that splits the store along its length, breaking the symmetry and defining the bright central space. While this dark band is used functionally to contain shelving and the main counter, reflective surfaces are carefully oriented along the line of demarcation between the dark and light zones to blur the limits of the overall space.

The sober and seemingly "undressed" space looks more like Philippe Dubuc's workshop than a usual retail store. The monochromatic palette harmonizes with the designer's creations; furthermore, the dust grey painted walls, polished concrete floors and minimal racks all relate to the industrial character of the site.

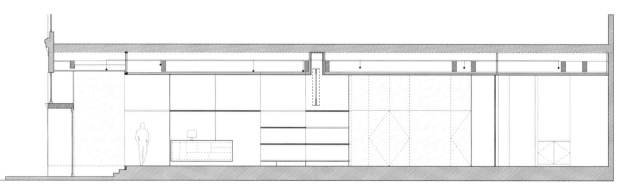

CIBOL in Beijing

SAKO Architects

Design: Keiichiro SAKO, Aya UNAGAMI / SAKO Architects
Client: Beijing Cibol Sanitary Co., Ltd.
Photography: Seiichi AOKI
Site: Beijing, China
Area: 85 sqm
Showroom

This is a showroom for terracotta bath articles in a shopping centre. When other brands mainly promote the bright family-style bathing room, the Black Box stands out from the White Box design of the gallery.

Under the spotlight, the white terracotta bath objects show off in the black space. Without any decoration, the terracotta bath articles are so pure, which builds up the relationship from one another between the product and visitor. The bath articles seem to be the artworks in the extraordinary showroom. The relationship between the object and human transfers from purchase into appreciation.

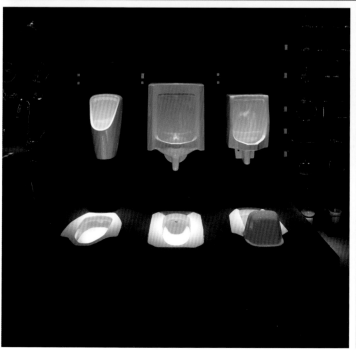

SPINNING OBJECTS
TORAFU ARCHITECTS

Design: TORAFU ARCHITECTS
Client: TOKYO Matsushima
Photography: Nobuaki Nakagawa / Yuki Ohmori / TORAFU
ARCHITECTS
Site: Tokyo, Japan
Area: 167 sqm
Showroom

This is a renovation project for a hotel fixtures showroom, which was required to display a large number of goods. If the number of items increased, the space needed to accommodate for the additions both spatially and visually. The designers aimed to design a strong space which could display a lot of the same kind of products effectively, and could bear new additions without changing the structure or interference to the design.

The designers proposed a series of "spinning" showcase, like dancers spinning or potter's wheel in motion. The items on display upon the circular cases become one with the "spinning objects". This creates an illusion like an after image.

When looking at the overall space, the "spinning objects" are expanded by reflecting on the ceiling and the floor. This unusual scene leaves a strong impression.

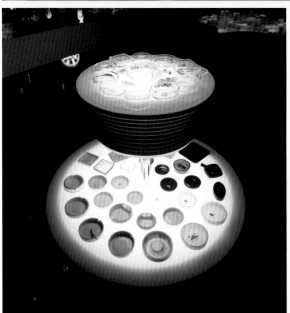

132 5. Issey Miyake
Tokujin Yoshioka

Design: Tokujin Yoshioka
Client: Issey Miyake
Photography: Yasuaki Yoshinaga, Nacása & Partners Inc.
Site: Tokyo, Japan
Area: 56 sqm
Retail store

The first store for "132 5. ISSEY MIYAKE" designed by Tokujin Yoshioka has been launched.

"132 5. ISSEY MIYAKE" is a new label and a new evolution of "A piece of Cloth" by Issey Miyake, based on the ideas of "Regeneration and Re-creation."

"Way of selling" is the concept of this space rather than the superficial interior design.

The clothes are displayed on five transparent torsos, which are strung down from the ceiling. Customers can access freely to the computer graphic images of the complicated process on the iPad installed in the store.

The display of the process from 2D to 3D makes it look like a Japanese Kimono store.

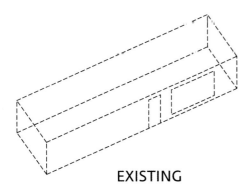

EXISTING

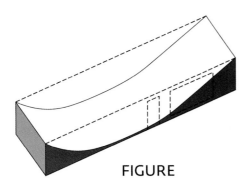

FIGURE

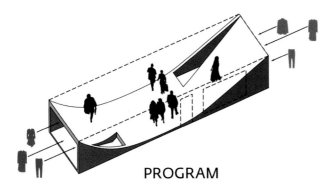

PROGRAM

Siki Im x LEONG LEONG Concept Store

LEONG LEONG

Design: LEONG LEONG
Client: Siki Im
Photography: David B. Smith, Pete Deevakul
Site: New York, USA
Area: 80 sqm
Retail store

The Siki Im x LEONG LEONG concept store completed as the final installation of Building Fashion at HL23 presented by BOFFO and Spilios Gianakopolous with PIN-UP Magazine and PROJECTNo.8. The concept store, developed in collaboration with fashion designer Siki Im, is the latest in a series of projects by LEONG LEONG that explore the transformation of a existing space through the insertion of a foreign figure or shape.

The structure, which is the former sales trailer for the HL23 building designed by Neil Denari, is filled end to end with large ramp-form that creates an unexpected gathering space with undefined programmatic possibilities. Soy-based spray foam is used to cover the interior and exterior of the structure creating a supple surface for inhabitation on which visitors are required to remove their shoes. Small niches and ledges are carved into the foam to create areas for display and seating. The clothes are embedded beneath the ramp on either end, encouraging visitors to explore the extents of the space and experience the clothes in very intimate environments.

Most of the time, if the grid has been set before the materials, the text and pictures will end up not fitting the grid: a situation that should be avoided.

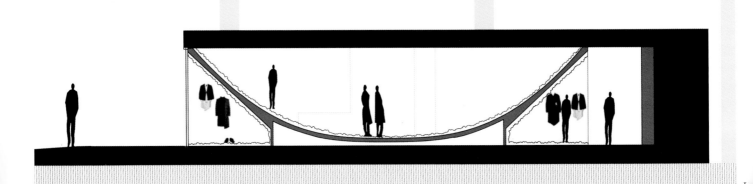

Richard Chai
Snarkitecture

Design: Snarkitecture
Client: Richard Chai
Photography: David B. Smith, Lexie Moreland, Snarkitecture
Site: New York, USA
Area: 53.5 sqm
Retail store

The Richard Chai store is a temporary retail installation created by Snarkitecture in collaboration with designer Richard Chai as part of the Building Fashion series at HL23, presented by Boffo and Spilios Gianakopoulos. Carved from the confines of an existing structure beneath the High Line, the installation envelops visitors within a glacial cavern excavated from a single material.

White architectural foam is cut by hand to produce erosions and extensions of the sculpted walls and ceiling to create a varied landscape for the display of Richard Chai's collection. The range of shelves, niches, hang bars and other moments embedded within the form encourage the designer's curatorial eye for display. At the close of the temporary installation, the material was returned to the manufacturer and recycled into rigid foam insulation.

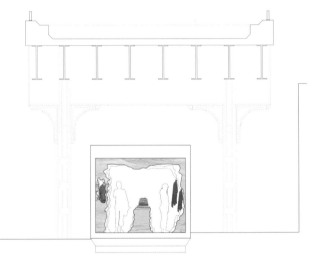

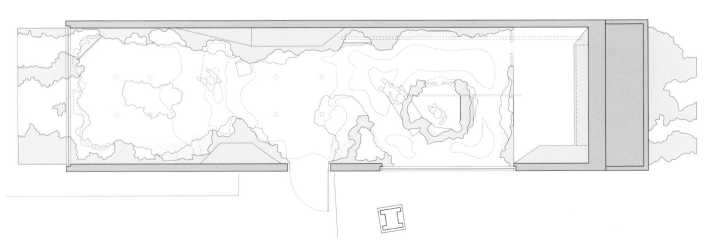

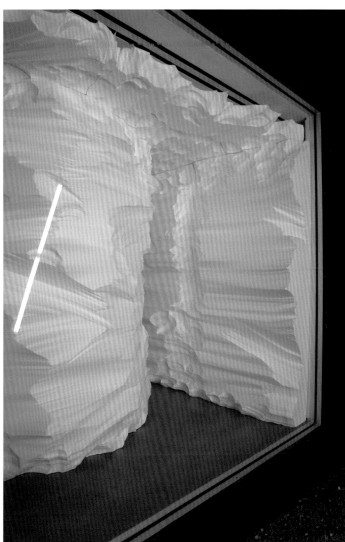

Camper Together

Tomás Alonso Design Studio

Design: *Tomás Alonso*
Client: *Camper*
Photography: *Sanchez & Montoro*
Site: *Covent Garden, London*
Area: *44 sqm*
Retail store

Since the great masters of the Modernist movement, no designer has been noted for his ability to bend a steel tube.

This apparently simple feat is actually quite difficult to perform with a natural flair, as Tomás Alonso does. Tubes, wood and color were all he needed to craft the furnishings for this new Camper store. Another simple flourish in the tile pattern creates an illusory three-dimensional effect on the walls.

All of the furnitures was designed and built specifically for the shop as part of a personal project Tomás Alonso has been working on for some time now, which is based on the formal and structural language that two materials as dissimilar as lacquer tubing and natural wood. In this case, white oak can create together. This language also extends to the stairs and the cash desk unit. The pieces were handcrafted at Tomás Alons's studio in London. Perhaps the most striking element is the large table with its accompanying chairs and benches, which take up most of the space. The ceramic lamps are also original designs. The wall cladding is a simple twist on the standard 10 x 10 cm square tile. If it is combined with three additional shapes, you can create all kinds of geometric patterns and designs in isometric perspective.

Air New Zealand "Clothes Hangar"
Gascoigne Associates Ltd.

Design: *Gascoigne Associates*
Client: *Air New Zealand*
Photography: *Katrina Rees, Rebecca Swan*
Site: *Auckland, New Zealand*
Area: *198 sqm*
Retail store

Air New Zealand's Clothes Hangar brief was to create a space that embodied Trelise Cooper's new uniform design direction and the Air New Zealand brand. The solution the designers came up with is a nod to a swept up eclectic kiwi Bach, providing staff a shopping experience like none other.

Gascoigne Associates designers Clark Pritchard and Theresa Ricacho consulted with Saatchi Design Worldwide to ensure the tie in with "the common thread" sub-brand idea and on the design of the wall decals, wallpaper and pictures.

The Clothes Hangar is located amongst factories and industrial warehouses, not the usual place where you would expect to discover a full service head to toe styling and grooming experience. However, a unique experience is exactly what Air New Zealand staff encounter once they pass through the blocked out front entrance and enter into a bright, clean and white space. On arrival staffs are greeted by the Clothes Hangar stylists. They can watch the welcome video on the LCD screen and view mannequins dressed in the new uniform, giving them an opportunity to see how the different uniform pieces can work together as a total wardrobe solution, as well as touch and feel the final fabrications.

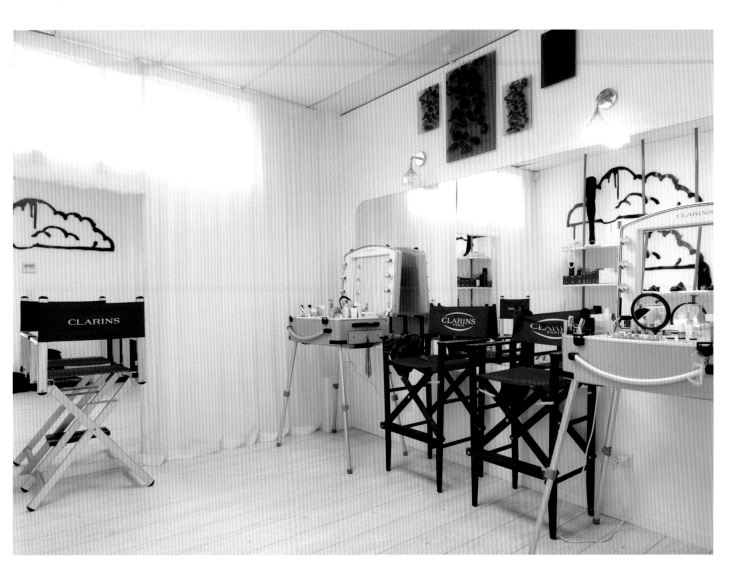

24 ISSEY MIYAKE
Nendo

Design: Nendo
Client: Issey Miyake
Photography: Daici Ano
Site: Tokyo, Japan
Area: 37 sqm
Showroom

Based on the concept of the Japanese convenience store, 24 ISSEY MIYAKE shops combine inexpensive prices, a large variety of colors and frequent changes in product lineup. The Miyake team wanted a new design concept for the 24 Issey Miyake shop in Shibuya's Parco shopping complex, which includes a display that specially features Miyake's new Bilbao bag.

The Bilbao bag has no set form. Instead, it settles depending on how it is placed. To match the bag, Nendo abandoned the standard, which was hard, flat and smooth fixtures found in most shops, and created a set of variable-height fixtures made of thin steel rods that stand like a field of prairie grass in the shop, with a similar vague, undefined shape like the bag. Shelving and hanger rods are also made of steel rods, in the 7 mm diameter common to all of the 24 Issey Miyake shop interiors. Supported by "points", rather than by surfaces or lines, the bags seem to waft in the air like flowers in a light breeze, creating the illusion of a field of flowers in the store.

CONTEMPORARY CRAFTSMANSHIP, by HERMÈS

CuldeSac™

Design: *CuldeSac*™
Client: *Hermès*
Photography: *CuldeSac*™
Site: *Madrid, Spain*
Area: *400 sqm*
Retail store

Like every season, Hermès launches its new collection of accessories inspired in the maison's brand values.

"Contemporary craftsmanship" highlights the brand's savoir-faire and the artisan's work through a contemporary prism portraying Hermès accessories as timeless objects of art.

Always surprising in its product launches, Hermès entrusted CuldeSac™ with the creativity for its A/W 2011 Accessories Presentation to the media.

Nine installations with artisan soul designed by the creative team devised a magical tour around the 400 sqm stately house, emulating the behind the scenes environment of the atelier, capturing the magic and values of the artisan work.

It is about time and balance, discipline and precision, craftsmanship and raw materials, curiosity, and so on. And the artisan's maxim is: bringing objects to life.

At the entrance, six marionettes around the table come to life recreating the fantasy of Gepetto, Pinocchio's artisan carpenter. Advancing towards the intimate space of the atelier, the male accessories unveil themselves among molds, unfinished pieces and remnants. The silk and cashmere carrés seem to float and gently rock to the sound of "The Nutcracker", a symphony of the artisan work and its tools.

The rhythm of discovery is paced, a metronome echoing the patience of the artisan shoemaker gains presence as the shoe collection slowly unveils among constant references to time and patience, precision and detail.

The final experience is filled with surprise, nostalgia and hidden treasures placed in those mythical music boxes invite to dream and remember.

RA antwerp and RA corderie paris

ra

Design: ra
Client: ra
Photography: Roman Hayat
Site: Belgium / Paris, France
Area: 800 sqm / 140 sqm
Retail store

Ra is an innovative platform and store in Antwerp, Belgium, a dynamic cultural open source fostering local and global networking.

Ra inspires and promotes, discovers and bridges emerging multidisciplinary talent with an international audience and market.

Ra is an area for displaying and producing a portfolio of products, site-specific projects, exhibitions, installations, performances, and hold events which promote and enrich the creative and cultural discourse.

Ra is a melting pot for fashion, art, design, music, books and fine food in a fluid experience. The ra concept store is an 800 sqm space, consisting of a 300 sqm fashion floor, an exhibition space, a book store, a music corner and a food corner. Due for completion in fall 2009, the space, formerly an art gallery, has been reconstructed and renovated, with respect to its historical architectural value.

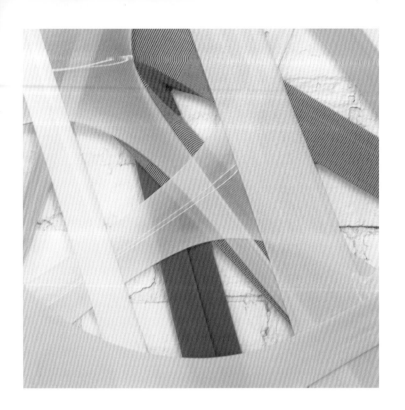

Arnsdorf Concept Store

Edwards Moore

Design: *Edwards Moore*
Client: *ARNSODRF*
Photography: *TONY GORSEVSKI*
Site: *Melbourne, Australia*
Area: *35 sqm*
Retail store

This temporary concept store is created for Australian fashion brand Arnsdorf, it features 154 pairs of tights stretched and wrapped around the retail space.

The small, cave-like space which popped up on Moor Street in Fitzroy, Melbourne for just three days in February 2011 provides an intimate setting for Arnsdorf's Opticks Collection, with soft hues and nude tones to complement the colors of the Opticks range. The fitout is inspired by crystalline forms, Superman's fortress of solitude and images of rocky landscapes. The fitout transforms an everyday, wearable item into a dramatic visual display to complement the sculptural Arnsdorf collection.

The cave-like structure is loosely inspired by Superman's Fortress of Solitude (superman 2) & Arnsdorf's Opticks collection.

The space is intended to be evocative of crystalline forms and rocky landscapes, aided by the reinterpretation of the humble ladies' stocking, stretched and wrapped en masse to envelope the room in earthen hues.

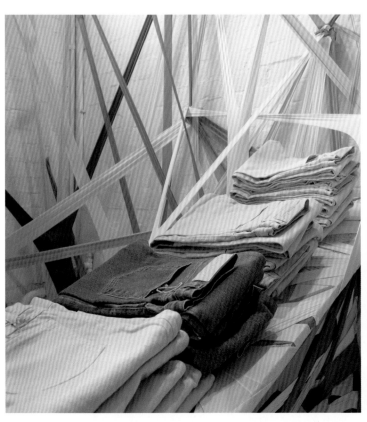

Trent Vioro

SHIMOKAWA Toru

Design: SHIMOKAWA Toru
Client: Trent
Photography: Hiroshi Mizusaki
Site: Fukuoka, Japan
Area: 110 sqm
Retail store

The client gave SHIMOKAWA Toru two contrary requests. One is open the facade in order to invite guests, the other is close the interior so that it can't be seen from the outside.

As a solution, the designer constructed the closed shop by wrapped it up, which has a wide opened facade with a hanging diagonal wall to the opposite angle. And also meets the fire department's requirements of the shopping mall.

And this inclined facade wall cross with elevator line made up a peculiar visual.

The facade wall is covered with hundreds of copper sheets. They are the same size as the stone plates on the floor. It will lose luster when touched by people who are interested in, and their color will turn reddish-brown (only copper and bronze) by oxidation and corroding as time goes by.

The reason why TRENT has established shops on the streets was that the designer intended to create their brand image by using materials such as copper, stones, concrete blocks and scaffold just like other TRENT shops did.

CANDIDO1859 - CLOTHES DEPT. STORE

LOLA, Local Office for Large Architecture

Design: RUTE BRAZAO, SANDRA CARITO RIBEIRO, RICCARDO CAVACIOCCHI
Client: CANDIDO1859
Photography: FRANCESCO PRATO
Site: Maglie, Italy
Area: 627 sqm
Retail store

The briefing defines the reformation of the final of Candido1859's three floors. Candido 1859 is one of the first fashion label stores opened in Southern Italy.

The floor is destined to be the Men's department and consists of a main commercial area, three separated mono label spaces, a "private" sales room and a storage area.

This floor was a later addition to the original 18th century building that was formerly a private residence whose structure is characterized by thick walls and high vaulted ceilings.

The challenge was to give a contemporary overhaul to this structurally marginalized space characterized by a very low ceiling and a central patio covering the lower main entrance hall.

The patio was raised to create the "private" sales room and its central round table with a reflective glass top works as a skylight for the lower spaces offering an extra value to the entrance on the ground floor.

The modular mirrored ceiling is composed of 8 repeated triangular elements heightens the space around the patio and entices the visitor before drawing her down a colored path of light. This reflection increases the space simultaneously fading the limits of shelves, hangers and exhibition elements.

The central patio can be used for events such as art exhibitions and private gatherings at the owner's discretion.

Customized elements such as hangers and mirrors can be easily added or removed and stored as needed.

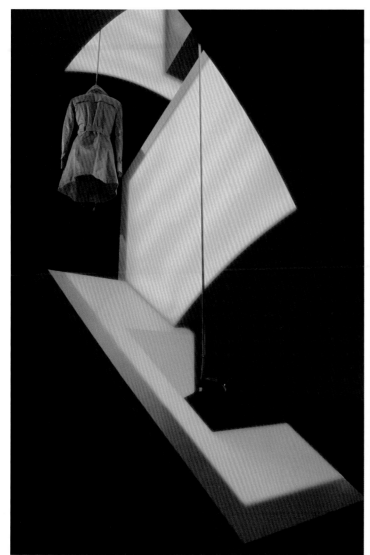

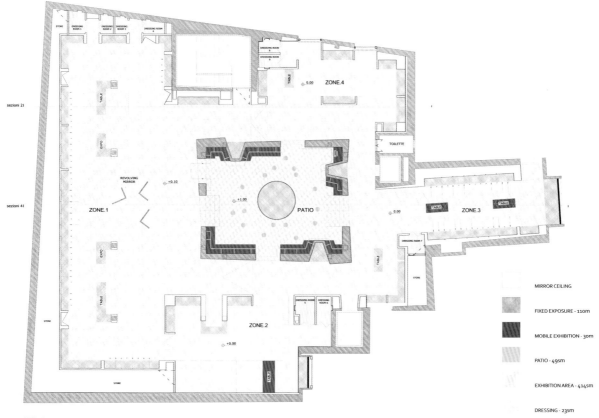

ZONE.1

REVOLVING MIRROR

EXPO

TABLE

EXPO

TABLE

STORE

STORE

sezioni 21

sezioni 41

STORE
DRESSING ROOM 1
DRESSING ROOM 2
DRESSING ROOM 3
DRESSING ROOM 4

DRESSING ROOM 5

DRESSING ROOM 6

TABLE

+0.00

ZONE.4

+0.10

+1.00

PATIO

TOILETTE

TABLE

+0.00

TABLE

TABLE

ZONE.3

DRESSING ROOM 7

STORE

TABLE

ZONE.2

DRESSING ROOM 8
DRESSING ROOM 9

+0.00

EXPO

MIRROR CEILING

FIXED EXPOSURE - 110m

MOBILE EXHIBITION - 30m

PATIO - 49sm

EXHIBITION AREA - 414sm

DRESSING - 23sm

GENERAL PLAN

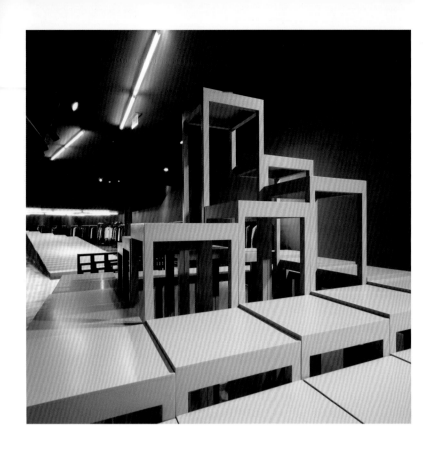

ALGEBRAIC VARIATIONS
FRANCESCO MONCADA

Design: FRANCESCO MONCADA
Client: B SILK
Photography: ALBERTO MONCADA
Site: Porto, Portugal
Area: 200 sqm
Retail store

"Algebraic Variations" is an installation designed for the interior refurbishment of Wrong Weather, a fashion and lifestyle store for the contemporary men in Porto, Portugal.

The renovation of a 200 square meter Wrong Weather concept store utilizes the existing space in a new way, in order to allow flexibility to display the items in multiple configurations, enabling the client to adapt to different seasons and collections.

The renovation of the shop is furnished with 206 modular structures, which occupy the centre of the shop. A sort of "Autoprogettazione" with modules, that allows the client's endless reconfiguration of the space according with the collection.

Each module with different proportion interacts with the space, with a cityscape inside it.

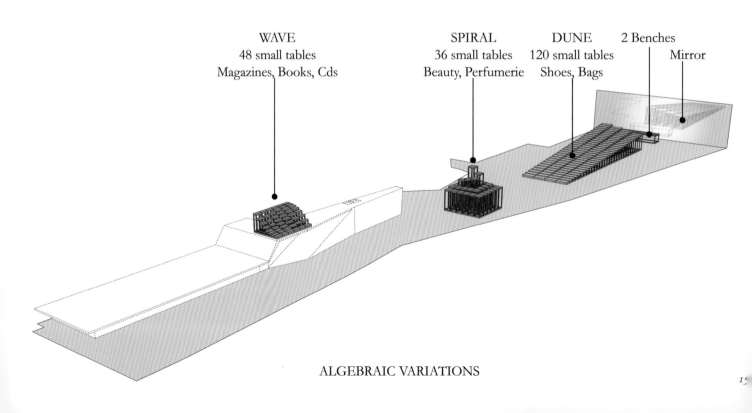

WAVE
48 small tables
Magazines, Books, Cds

SPIRAL
36 small tables
Beauty, Perfumerie

DUNE
120 small tables
Shoes, Bags

2 Benches
Mirror

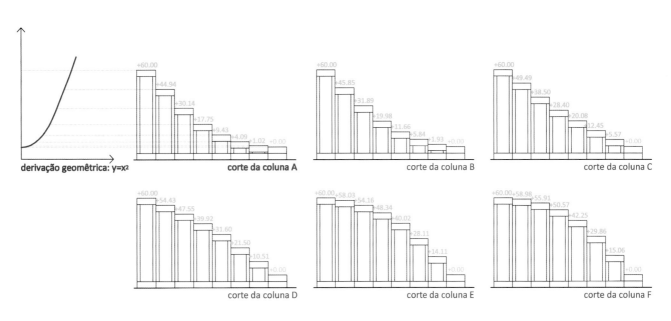

derivação geomêtrica: y=x²

+60.00
+44.94
+30.14
+17.75
+9.43
+4.09 +1.02 +0.00

corte da coluna A

+60.00
+45.85
+31.89
+19.98
+11.66
+5.84 +1.93 +0.00

corte da coluna B

+60.00
+49.49
+38.50
+28.40
+20.08
+12.45
+5.57 +0.00

corte da coluna C

+60.00
+54.43
+47.55
+39.92
+31.60
+21.50
+10.51
+0.00

corte da coluna D

+60.00 +58.03
+54.16
+48.34
+40.02
+28.11
+14.11
+0.00

corte da coluna E

+60.00 +58.98
+55.91
+50.57
+42.25
+29.86
+15.06
+0.00

corte da coluna F

PUMA HOUSE TOKYO
Nendo

Design: *Nendo*
Client: *PUMA*
Photography: *Daici Ano*
Site: *Tokyo, Japan*
Area: *330 sqm*
Retail store

The new Puma House Tokyo is located in the city's Aoyama design district. It is the first time that Puma House Tokyo combines the brand's press room and event space into one space. Puma House Tokyo is a multipurpose space that can be used for exhibitions, events, fittings, product launches and other media events. It is also available for rentals.

For Nendo's design, they placed "staircases" that climb around the existing features around the space like vines. But these staircases are not for people to climb. Rather, they function as display stands for PUMA's sneakers and as a compositional element that gives the space a special character. The resulting effect is a strong reminder that we exercise our bodies' daily going up and down stairs, and has a visual connection with stadium stairs and podiums too, to bring in PUMA's important relationship with sports. The stairs bring a sense of movement to the interior, enabling a three-dimensional product display that fully uses its space and allows visitors to experience PUMA's worldview.

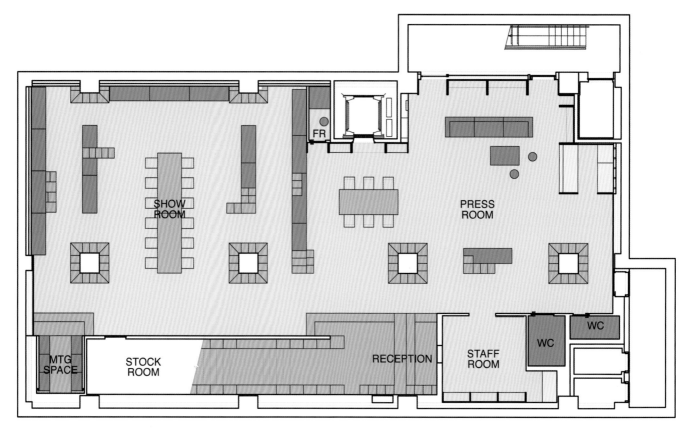

PLEATS PLEASE ISSEY MIYAKE BANGKOK SIAM DISCOVERY CENTER

KEISUKE FUJIWARA DESIGN OFFICE

Design: KEISUKE FUJIWARA
Client: ISSEY MIYAKE lnc.
Photography: SATOSHI ASAKAWA
Site: BANGKOK, THAILAND
Area: 138 sqm
Retail store

This is the first store for PLEATS PLEASE ISSEY MIYAKE opened in Thailand. One of the symbolic designs is the column, which is located through the white entrance. It has three different sizes of round shelves, and one of them has an automatic rotating function. It brings out the lightness of PLEATS PLEASE's clothes. The hanger fixture which is the extension of the barrel vault gives a tension and lighthearted mood to the customers. It also plays the most important role as a function, since the barrel vault can transform itself into a necessity, such as a wall or a shelf fixture. The barrel vaults vaguely divide the space into three different zones.

The designer attempts to design the space that gives an easy understanding to the customers about characteristics of the products, such as material, color, flatness and lightness. They are attempted to be expressed in the interior design. Every product is created from the perfect exploring that does not forgive the compromise. As a result, they have dignity and sympathy. This must be the reason why "PLEATS PLEASE ISSEY MIYAKE" attracts the world. It has been an important role for the designers to express them through the space. The significant point is to be able to expand in Thailand as well.

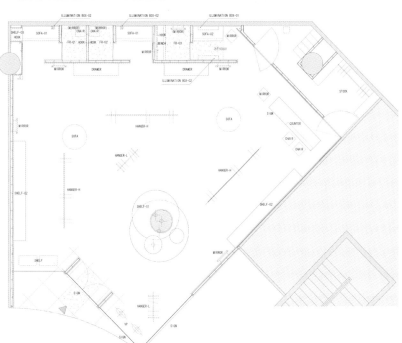

Placebo Pharmacy

Klab Architecture, Konstantinos Labrinopoulos

Design: *Xara Marantidou, Enrique Ramirez, Mark Chapman, Konstantinos Labrinopoulos*
Client: *Private*
Photography: *P. Kokkinias*
Site: *Athens, Greece*
Area: *600 sqm*
Retail store

The design process for this large (600m²) supralocal pharmacy forced the designers to shift their viewpoint and come up with a virtual building, a placebo pharmacy. The octagonal shape of the existing structure was re-formed into a cylinder in order to create a spiral which seeks to converse with the rapid motion on Vouliagmenis Avenue, the urban artery on which the building stands. The panels of the facade are perforated using Braille, which both alludes to the system's use on pharmaceutical packaging and boosts visibility by allowing the light to find its way into the interior. The new facade also protects the interior while acting as a lure for passers-by. Inside, the product display mirrors the circular frontage, while a ramp up to the upper level extends the dynamism of the exterior spiral into the interior space.

The Pharmacy is arranged over two floors, the ground floor is the primary shop space with an upper mezzanine floor consisting of ancillary office space used as a temporary surgery for visiting health professionals.

The pharmacy is arranged in plan in a radial pattern with the main cashier's desk acting as the focal point. The product displays fan out from this focal point giving the cashier the ability to view the whole pharmacy from this central area. The drug dispensary, preparation areas and toilets are also arranged off this radial pattern. This pattern gives a natural flow to the space and allows light go deep into the center of the plan at all times throughout the day.

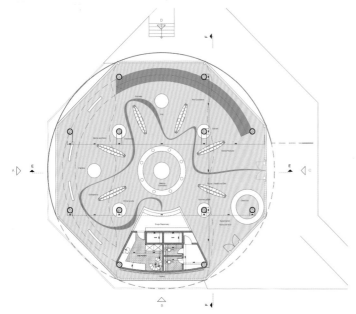

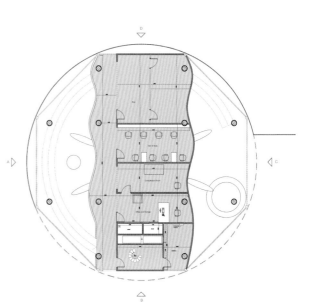

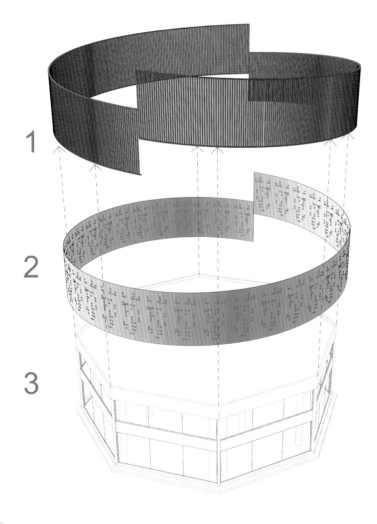

1

2

3

3.1 Phillip Lim-Seoul
LEONG LEONG

Design: LEONG LEONG
Client: 3.1 Phillip Lim and Shinsegae International
Photography: Iwan Baan, Leong Leong Architecture
Site: Seoul, Korea
Area: 585 sqm
Retail store

The flagship store designed by Leong Leong for 3.1 Phillip Lim is located in Cheongdam-Dong, Seoul's premiere fashion district. In a period of eight months, Leong Leong designed and oversaw the construction of the 550-square-meter store in an existing four-story building.

This project is a single store within 3.1 Phillip Lim's global roll-out campaign, which will include many international locations. Aware of the inevitable repetition that is necessary for such a commercial expansion, we thought of the typology of a flagship store as being characterized by the simultaneous need for sameness and difference. Typically, the consistent repetition of brand traits is necessary to reinforce an identity, while novelty can refresh the aura and desire for the brand. In this particular case the client, a relatively new fashion house launched in 2004, emphasized the need to establish a legible consistency in order to unify the different existing stores in New York, Los Angeles, and Tokyo.

GROUND FLOOR PLAN

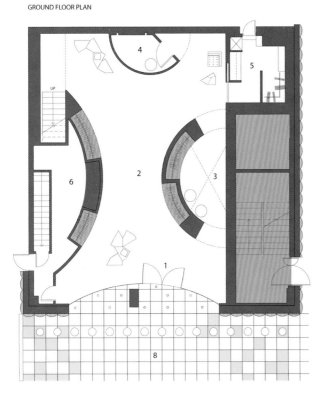

UPPER FLOOR PLAN

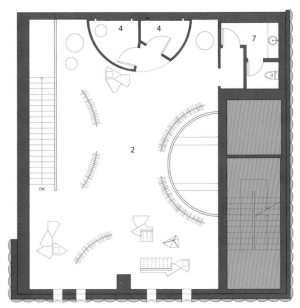

1m   2m

1   ENTRANCE
2   MAIN RETAIL
3   RETAIL
4   CHANGING ROOM
5   POINT OF SALE
6   STORAGE
7   RESTROOM
8   COURTYARD

PANEL 0 PANEL 1 PANEL 2 PANEL 3 PANEL 4 PANEL 5 PANEL 6

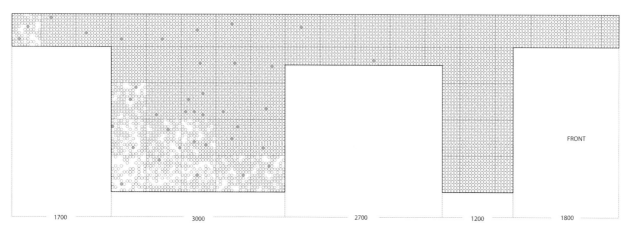

1700   3000   2700   1200   1800

FRONT

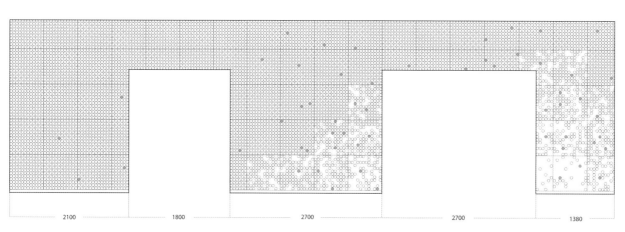

2100   1800   2700   2700   1380

PANEL TYPES

P1   P2   P3   P4   P5

Kyoto Silk
Keiichi Hayashi Architect

Design: Keiichi Hayashi
Client: Kyoto Silk
Photography: Yoshiyuki Hirai
Site: Kyoto, Japan
Area: 67.58 sqm
Retail store

Kyoto Silk, a beauty cosmetic shop, is located in the centre of Kyoto, which is a famous cultural city in Japan. The project was to convert a "Machiya", a Japanese traditional wooden townhouse, into a small shop. The building was required to be reinforced because the original building was deteriorating rapidly and it did not have enough strength to meet the safety standards. Therefore, on the ground floor of the two stories, thin steel frames were fixed on the inside of the original wooden frames. And on the first floor, a plywood structure was used on the floor to keep the horizontal rigidity.

In this project, Keiichi Hayashi focused on the way that functions as a beauty cosmetic shop could be complimented by the space limitations of this "Machiya".

The most important thing for this plan of a sales place is to make the products clear for the customers. (Not simply as beauty display, but making it clear to the customer exactly what the product is.) A homogeneous, hard optical environment and simple shelves were considered so that the products never look exaggerated. The courtyard is placed at the back of the sales space and is the space for the guests and the staff to take a rest. At the same time, it is the space to take in the small nature of the store. The space is able to be accessed directly through from the street. These relations are exactly the same as the original "Machiya". The first floor of this building is used as an office and gallery.

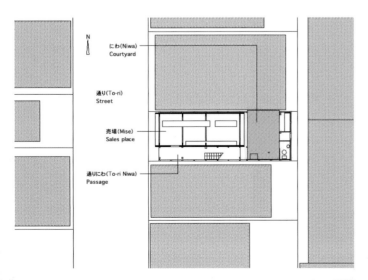

N

にわ(Niwa)
Courtyard

通り(To-ri)
Street

売場(Mise)
Sales place

通りにわ(To-ri Niwa)
Passage

1階平面
Ground Floor

JEANSWEST in Suzhou

SAKO Architects

Design: Keiichiro SAKO, Nobutoshi HARA / SAKO Architects
Client: JeansWest international(HK)LTD.
Photography: Zhonghai SHEN
Site: Suzhou, China
Area: 340 sqm
Retail store

This is a flagship store for the clothing brand JEANSWEST under which there are more than 2500 branches in China. The store is located in the crowded walking street. Because of the weather in Suzhou, the door leaves are opened all the year round. The target of the store is young, and its design aims is to create a diversified space to attract the passers-by.

There is no doubt that the way of showing the products on the wall will be adopted basing on the relation between the volume of passengers and the volume of goods. Filling the wall with products is a traditional method which can help to show more products to customers. However, the designers did not adopt it, instead, the designers divided the wall into couple of units to create a diffluent space, to make the L-form plane vertical towards the axial direction, and divide it every 600mm. The space is big enough to show the complete garment, and even the vertical air conditioner of the smallest size can be contained. Every unit slopes by 5 degree and 10 degree respectively, which looks like the wave flowing in the air. When walking inside, people can see the ceiling ups and downs in the air, by comparison, the exhibit on the wall seems to be the loom, which creates an illusion. The L shape space has attracted a lot of customers to walk inside and find out more about the store.

The Archive
k&k architects

Design: *k&k architects*
Client: *Carteco*
Photography: *Anastasia Adamaki*
Site: *Thessaloniki, Greece*
Area: *21 sqm*
Retail store

In January 2008, k&k architects were commissioned by Carteco, a Greek company specializing in the retail of architectural materials, to design a creative working place for architects and designers, with a material's library. The space should reflect the company's devotion to architecture and design, as well as its wish to continuously support creative young minds. The Archive is available 24 hours a day, 7 days a week with the use of a personalized entrance card. The Archive is located in a ground floor store in the center of Thessaloniki, Greece's second largest city. The possible expansion of the brand in other cities was a parameter taken into consideration from the beginning of the design process.

The architectural concept is the creation of a "shell" through the bending of a single flat pattern. The idea behind this synthesis is the creation of a space that resembles to an architectural model, the par excellence architectural design tool. The result is a folded surface whose folds form the necessary furniture, embody lights and create space for exhibiting materials.

White painted osb boards, mounted on a light metal structure, are used for the construction of the surface. The surrounding walls and the ceiling of the space are painted black allowing the structure to stand out more effectively. Two custom made "barcode" bookcases (inspired by the company's logo) were designed to accommodate catalogues from numerous companies that specialize in architectural materials. One of them also functions as a filter providing visual privacy from the busy street outside. The whole structure is placed within a small distance from the glass facade, making space for furniture display or periodical store-front exhibitions. A series of selected architectural events are presented on-site through the year, in order to constantly revive the interest of the Archive's creative members.

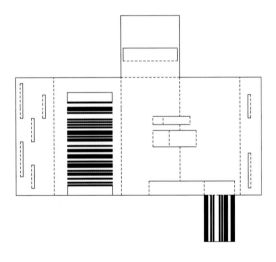

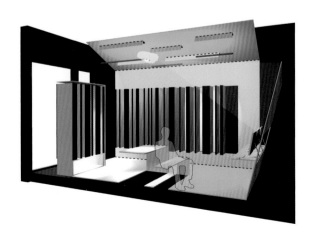

PRESS HERE
FOR A 30 MINUTE
ENLIGHTMENT

18

PRESS HERE
FOR A 30 MINUTE
ENLIGHTMENT

PRESS HERE
FOR A 30 MINUTE
ENLIGHTMENT

STEP HERE

Camper @ BBB
Nendo

Design: *Nendo*
Client: *Camper*
Site: *Barcelona, Spain*
Showroom

The exhibition design for Spanish footwear maker Camper's display at Bread & Butter Barcelona, the international street and urban wear tradeshow.

The collection's theme "Imagination Walks" refers to the way that each pair of shoes has its own story, and provokes the creativity of its wearer. The designers decided to express the theme with an exhibition built entirely out of books, which was a classic symbol of narrative and creativity. Demarcated by bookshelves, and full "stacks of books" for stands and stools, the exhibition space became a virtual library of footwear stories.

GREGORY
TOKYO STORE
TORAFU ARCHITECTS

Design: TORAFU ARCHITECTS
Client: GREGORY
Photography: Daici Ano / TORAFU ARCHITECTS
Site: Tokyo, Japan
Area: 64.4 sqm
Retail store

Outdoor apparel maker Gregory opened its first road-side store on Harajuku's Cat Street.

The first floor carries casual items such as bags, while professional mountain climbing gears can be found on the second floor. Since the existing building is located in the corner of a Y-intersection, it had no depth. The designers had to make attempts at exhibiting a variety of products, as well as giving adequate space for stock items in the limited site area.

The designers envisioned various settings, such as a ragged mountain, a dense forest and an Alpine hut to rest in, all of which Gregory backpacks have been utilized in. They set the hut behind the entrance's glass wall, which functions as the store's line up display on shelves that completely cover the wall. The backpacks lodged between the partition boards remind people of a rock climbing scene.

INHABITANT STORE TOKYO
TORAFU ARCHITECTS

Design: TORAFU ARCHITECTS
Client: INHABITANT
Photography: Daici Ano
Site: Tokyo, Japan
Area: 224.5 sqm
Retail store

The INHABITANT STORE TOKYO opened in Harajuku's Cat Street as the lifestyle / sport brand's flagship store. "Playfulness" and "Japaneseness" are the embodiment of INHABITANT's freestyle expression of modern Japanese taste and which inspired the designers to envision a space thriving with the spontaneity of a casual stroll through the area known as "the back of Harajuku".

On each of the two floors, long plates cross diagonally the display areas with fitting rooms and counters positioned at a comfortable distance from them. Shoppers are greeted by a long plate on the first floor that can be used as a table to put articles on display, work or serve as a catwalk for special events. The edge of the plate becomes a step to the stairwell leading to the second floor where a suspended plate emerging from the wall welcomes customers like an overhead gate before extending diagonally into the display area holding hanger racks on its bottom side and multi-directional spotlights on its top to showcase the hexagonal tortoise-shell patterns spreading like clouds on the ceiling. Artist Asao Tokolo elaborated two patterns, whose every edge will always match every other, which can be seen encroaching on the floors, ceilings, walls and columns all over the store.

By capitalizing on the mutual relationship of the smaller units composing it, we strived to create a space that would in turn blend in with the small boutiques and residences that make up "the back of Harajuku".

minä perhonen
"Rainwear In /
Rainwear Out"
TORAFU ARCHITECTS

Design: TORAFU ARCHITECTS
Client: minä perhonen
Photography: Daici Ano
Site: Tokyo, Japan
Area: 77.8 sqm
Retail shop

This is minä perhonen's third temporary installation to be held at "The Stage", located on the 1st floor of the Isetan Department Store in Shinjuku. The year's theme, "Rainwear In / Rainwear Out", revolved around a booth shaped like a house to highlight the "inside" and "outside" experience of a rainy day. The booth's walls prominently featured minä perhonen's "sunny rain" textile pattern, while chairs shaped like rain drops and mirrors shaped like puddles, complete the picture for a fun day in the rain.

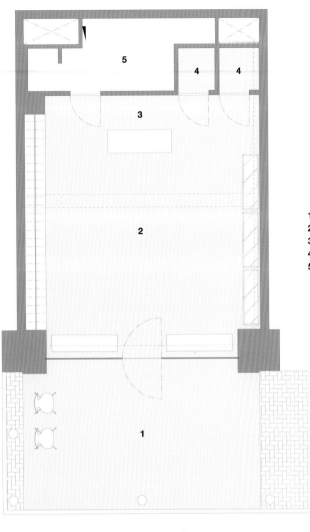

Trent Ohashi
SHIMOKAWA Toru

Design: SHIMOKAWA Toru
Client: Trent
Photography: Hiroshi Mizusaki
Site: Fukuoka, Japan
Area: 43 sqm
Retail store

1 Approach
2 Display
3 Counter
4 Fitting space
5 Staff room

This is a lady's apparel store. Although the floor area is small, the designers focused on utilizing the area for common use next to the entrance.

Laying both areas with turf works inside and outside with sashless glasses, the continuation makes the area outstanding and feels bigger and wider.

OPUS SHOP
Paradox Studio

Design: *Paradox Studio*
Client: *OPUS International*
Photography: *Benjamin Chou*
Site: *Taiwan, China*
Area: *10.5 sqm*
Retail store

OPUS is a brand specializing in purse hangers, which can be placed securely on the edge of the table to hang your purse, hence free up space at the table and on the seats, and free up your hands for more activities. OPUS Taipei is the first shop for the brand and was designed to be a multi-purpose space that can be used for meetings, product launches as well as a retail store.

OPUS Taipei is located in the city's fashion district. The previous use for this location was a garage and the space was converted into a small storefront during the economic recession.

The store is merely 2.3 meters wide and 4.5 meters long, which is about 10.5 square meters and is a very petite space. To overcome the size limitation of the store, Paradox Studio designed a perspective illusion by painting yellow color blocks (using OPUS' signature color) on white walls to create the impression of a deeper and wider space. The rhythmic yellow blocks run along the two opposite walls of the store and converged into a horizontal line on the back wall which is highlighted with a clock custom-designed by them.

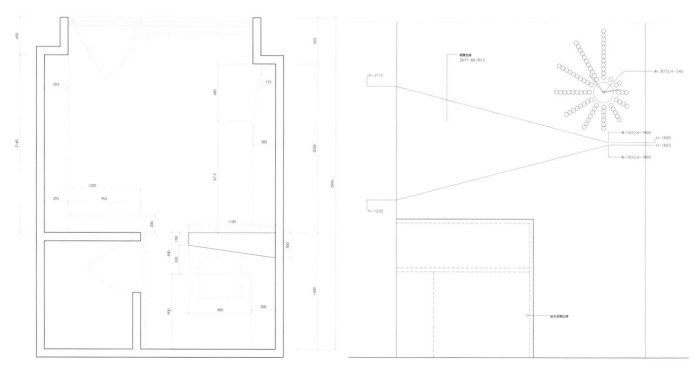

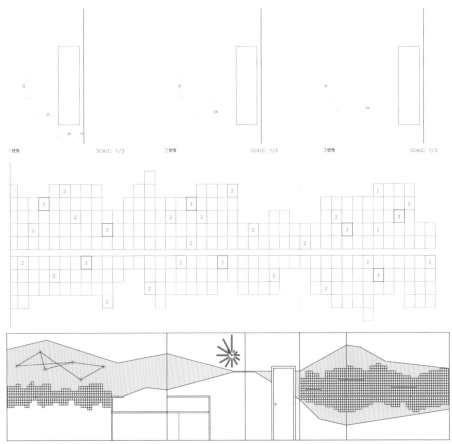

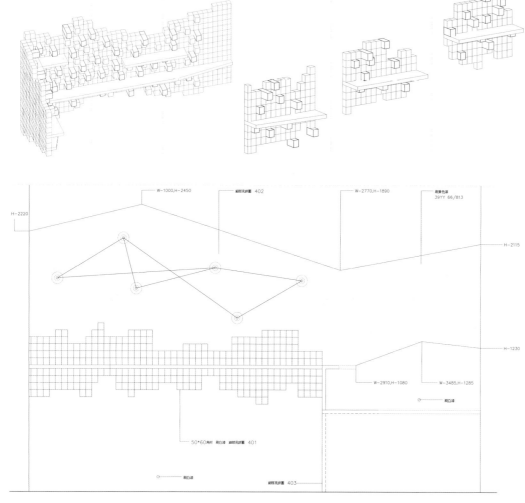

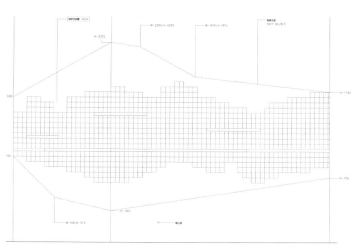

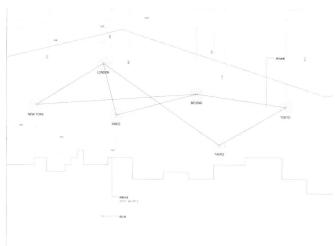

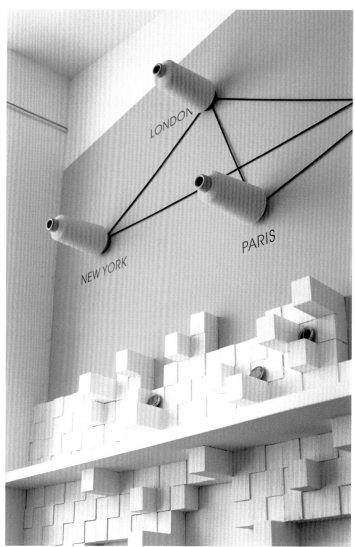

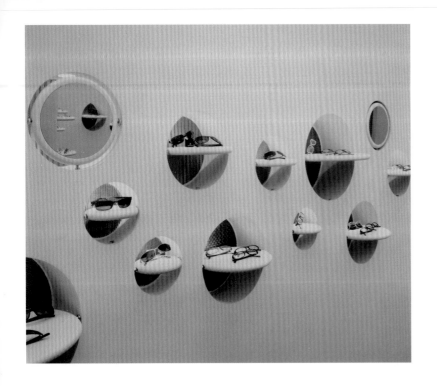

RODENSTOCK
BRILLE GINZA

Endo Shuhei Architect Institute

Design: *Endo Shuhei Architect Institute*
Client: *RODENSTOCK*
Photography: *Nacasa & Partners Inc.*
Site: *Tokyo, Japan*
Area: *54 sqm*
Retail store

This is the first store for RODENSTOCK in Japan, a highly reputed German glassmaker. The store is located in Ginza, Tokyo, and therefore, a high quality space was required to reflect the values of the RODENSTOCK brand and its customers.

The space was constructed of strait and curved plaster surfaces covered in transparent circular patterns. Set in this pattern, are rotating circular panels of varying sizes. These panels can be turned in order to act as display shelves or mirrors. Also, the ceiling has been layered with sheets of cracked and frosted glasses.

These systems create a space with required flexibility to accommodate a variety of customers, as everyone has a different face. Moreover, the customers can feel the change of the space as they move inside the store. These design aspects make the space looks larger than it actually is, while displaying the items of RODENSTOCK.

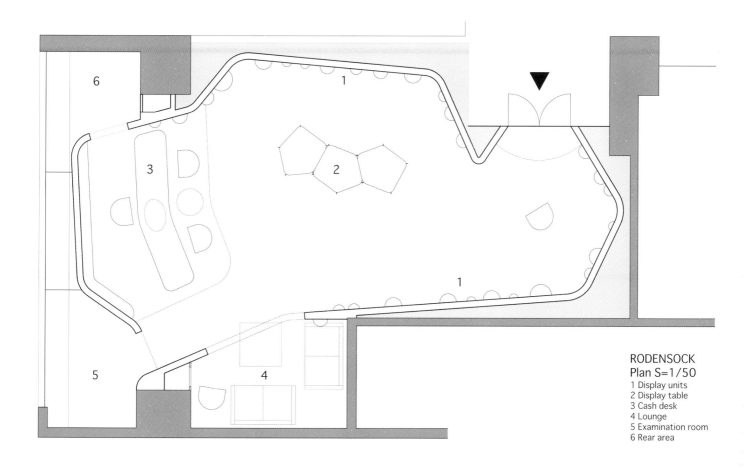

RODENSOCK
Plan S=1/50
1 Display units
2 Display table
3 Cash desk
4 Lounge
5 Examination room
6 Rear area

Firefly Squid
O.F.D.A arcchitects studio

Design: Taku Sakaushi O.F.D.A
Client: Tabuse
Photography: Hiroshi Ueda
Site: Tokyo, Japan
Area: 54 sqm
Restaurant

Building in a narrow plot, the small Italian restaurant Firefly Squid is in the business district in Tokyo. As the site was surrounded by facades of tall contiguous similar flats, our strategy was to insert and crack the pathway like a garden through the site, using the merit of such small area due to the limited budget. By dividing the site narrow into two lanes, a proper width for counter seats and path-garden was provided at the same time. A horizontal ribbon window opened below waist height gives the customers a garden view.

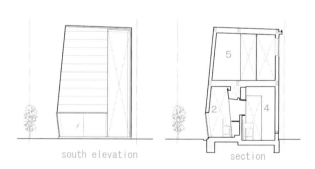

south elevation   section

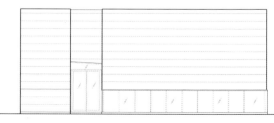

west elevation

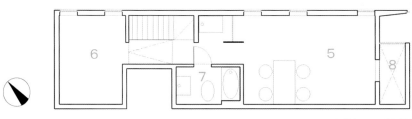

2nd Floor PLAN

1   entrance
2   counter seats
3   box seats
4   kitchin
5   party room
6   warehouse
7   bathroom
8   void space
9   pathway garden

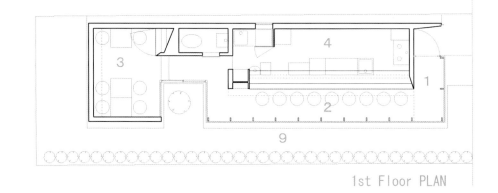

1st Floor PLAN

+ green
sinato Inc.

Design: sinato Inc.
Client: Dream Studio Co.,Ltd.
Photography: Toshiyuki Yano
Site: Tokyo, Japan
Area: 111.53 sqm
Restaurant

An organic restaurant is located on Jiyu Street, which is a short walk from Komazawa Park, one of the biggest parks in Tokyo. It has three functions: a takeout, an organic food shop and a restaurant.

The most distinctive feature of the premises lies in its floor level is a 1.61m below-the-ground level entrance, and its premises' height is 4.39m.

To study the arrangement of these three functions in such a unique space was the beginning for Sinato's design. They arranged the restaurant on the half underground floor, the takeout place in front of the entrance has the same level as the ground and the shop place diagonally away from the takeout place. Instead of hiding the restaurant from the entrance, it gets sunlight on the restaurant floor from opening facade.

There are 3 floor levels for each function, people can move up and down in this space. In the lower space, you can slightly feel the border of the white wall above your head, and it's quite different from the plan of the restaurant floor partitioned by the brick wall. The angle of the brick wall turns a lot of times to form an inside hall space, a private room, a kitchen and a storeroom on the outside, which is between the brick wall and original wall.

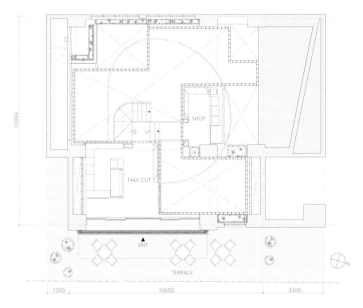

upper level plan : 1/150

lower level plan : 1/150

Niseko Look Out Cafe

design spirits co. , ltd.

Design: *design spirits co. , ltd. , Yuhkichi Kawai*
Client: *YTL Hotels*
Photography: *Toshihide Kajiwara*
Site: *Hokkaido, Japan*
Area: *172 sqm*
Café

Look out Café is located on the top of the mountain, and it is impossible to reach it by a car or ski-lifts during the off-season. Therefore, there were many times, the designers and the constructors had to walk, hike, and climb over another slope to get down of the site. Also, the materials were carried by Caterpillar vehicle with a carrier attached to it.

In the meantime, construction workers had to climb up and down the mountain on foot if the carrier is fully-occupied with materials.

When it rained, the designers were prohibited to climb the mountain as there was a possibility of land sliding.

In Japan, the daytime of autumns and winters is shorter than nighttime. Sunset begins at 4 in the evening in despite of sunny day or cloudy day. In addition, strong winds also come as a result of frigid condition. These forced them to leave the site before sunset in order to avoid any unfortunate consequences. As a result, construction progress was unable to proceed as scheduled.

However, the progress of construction is always depends on the changes of situation. Fortunately, it was a warm winter this year as snowfall came late, and construction could be carried out until the end of November.

The project was completed by early December, with a grand opening for Look out Café.

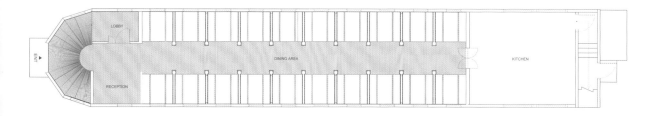

Asian Sweets and Cafe Koki

Akira Koyama + KEY OPERATION INC.

Design: *Akira Koyama + KEY OPERATION INC.*
Client: *Private*
Photography: *Nacasa & Partners*
Site: *Ishikawa, Japan*
Area: *92.58 sqm*
Café

Unusually for Japan where buildings are readily demolished with new ownership, Akira Koyama by Key Operation Inc. makes use of a relatively old building built in 1971. Café Koki is located in the trend-setting Tatemachi shopping district of Kanazawa City. How to combine new with old is a challenge that young Japanese architects increasingly face in post-bubble Japan. While many of them choose to rid traces of the past in such a situation, Koyama manages to subtly incorporate the existing features to create a modern space that is not entirely cut off from the past.

The new shop's facade is painted in rustic red to recall Shanghai. It refers to the red brick buildings that the French built when they owned part of the city during the 19th century. Some of the steel plates, which have been carefully arranged to reinforce the brick motif, are perforated to let the light in. The long eaves, also painted in rustic red, on the other hand, seems to recall the exaggerated eaves associated with Buddhist temples, a religion which was originally imported from China into Japan. The reference to the distant past does not end there. Nearly half of the facade is cut out and fitted with a large piece of glazing, which is of course part of the Modernist architectural lexicon of lightness and transparency, but more importantly here, such a setup helps to create the illusion of oku or depth, which is very much part of the traditional Japanese building approach.

Original features, such as the curved windows, have been put to good use. Inspired by their curvature, and to compliment the delicate softness of the sweets, the architect rounded off sharp corners where the ceilings and walls meet and created the playful twirls in the forms of steps downstairs. An intriguing display of light moreover comes alive at night, via these curved windows, with an additional layer of perforated steel on the facade. Koyama's inclusive approach to modernity works along with, rather than against, the past. Just as the sweets sold at Café Koki are promoted to have health benefits, the tradition is cleverly weaved in this space to suit the modern taste.

INDEX

CuldeSac™ / p.134-137

CuldeSac™ is more than a studio. It's a creative lab, a space for collaboration on different fields of expertise. It was founded as a melting pot for professionals to dialogue and exchange knowledge. Founded in 2002, CuldeSac™ is a team of more than 40 people, headed by Alberto Martinez and Pepe Garcia (CuldeSac™ Product & Interiors and founders), Juan Poveda and Xavi Sempere (CuldeSac™ Branding) and Garen Moreno and Sophie von Schönburg (CuldeSac™ Experience). Despite the fact that its founder members studied at the Royal College of Art in London, the studio decided to settle in Valencia. The city's relaxed atmosphere inspirates a place of interdisciplinary work on spaces, product, branding, events, communication and PR.

www.culdesac.es

design spirits co. , ltd. / p.224-227

Co-founder & Chief Designer Yuhkichi Kawai was born in Tokyo, Japan in 1967. Graduated from Keio University Law dept in 1992 and Kuwasawa Design Institute Space Design dept in 1997. He established design spirits co.,ltd. in 2003.

He won Silver Award of JCD, Nomination Award of IAI Biennial Awards, and Best 100 of JCD in 2010.

www.design-spirits.com

Edwards Moore / p.142-143

Edwards Moore is a creative practice born from varied design backgrounds and driven by a belief in the art of architecture. We developed an identity system that explored the interplay between the two directors, Ben Edwards and Juliet Moore.

Each typographic expression was informed by emotive characteristics that defined the partnership: serious, playful, energetic, precise, and learning.

www.edwardsmoore.com

Electric Dreams AB / p.040-043

Electric Dream is a Stockholm-based architecture / design studio formed by Joel Degermark and Cathrina Frankander in 2006. Major projects include vour vtrrriple interior concepts for Monki, permanent exhibition for the Vase Museum, the Pleasant Bar and Weekday Malmo. Our designs are much about story telling and themes, a fascination of playful exaggeration. We like things that are too colorful, too weird, too beautiful, too dark, too many. Our design becomes surreal because it is a lot about shifting scales, bringing two familiar things together to create the unfamiliar, and playing with visual effects11.

www.electricdreams.se

Endo Shuhei Architect Institute / p.210-213

Endo Shuhei was born in Shiga Prefecture in 1960. Obtained a master's degree at Kyoto University of Art in 1986. Established Shuhei Endo Architect Institute in 1988, and was the professor at the international summer academy in Salzburg in 2004 and currently professor at Graduate School of Kobe University.

Endo Shuhei won AIJ Annual Architectural Design Commendation 2008 and Prize of Architecture Governor of Osaka in 2008. Prize of Architecture Governor of Osaka and ARCASIA Award in 2007. AIJ Annual Architectural Design Commendation 2006 and Architecture Award in Chuubu in 2006.

www.paramodern.com

FRANCES RIFE STUDIO / p.066-069

Interior and Industrial designer was born in Sant Sadurni d'Anoia (Barcelona, Spain) in 1969. His professional career began as an undergraduate through independent commissions for various Design and Architecture studios while at the same time taking on his own projects.

In 1994, after several years of training in his field, he established his own studio in Barcelona. From here he directs his team with a fusion of different disciplines. His projects range from Interior to Industrial Design, both containing commercial and private projects.

His design principle is based on the search for spatial order and geometric proportion.

www.rife-design.com

FRANCESCO MONCADA / p.154-157

Francesco Moncada received his M.Arch. from the University of Palermo, Italy in 2004. He has lived and worked in Spain, UK, Portugal, The Netherlands, Norway, and Dubai. His most notable experience comes from Foreign Office Architects in London, and OMA/Rem Koolhaas in Rotterdam.

His projects have been published in Wallpaper, Wired, Frame, Interni, Case d'Abitare, Ottagono, Attitude, Arquitectura & Construccao, Perspective Hong Kong, Dezeen, Designboom, Archdaily, Plataforma Arquitectura and in various books about interiors. His work has been exhibited at the London Festival Architecture for the "Wallpaper Architects Directory 2010" and in EXPO 2010 in Shanghai in the Italian Pavilion. At the moment beside his office, Francesco Moncada is collaborating with OMA/Rem Koolhaas in Rotterdam.

www.francescomoncada.com

Gascoigne Associates Ltd. / p.128-131

Gascoigne Associates is a multi-disciplinary design and consultancy office that integrates architecture with interior design, lighting design, and retail branding services.

Gascoigne specialise in creating new retail brands and re-imaging of existing ones. Design services are provided for a wide range of projects, both nationally and internationally. Clients include many of the most successful retailers from Australasia as well as several multinational corporates such as Toyota and Westfield. Current project budgets range from $100k to $95m. Gascoigne is currently designing and rolling out projects throughout Australia and New Zealand as well as selected projects in Asia.

Completed works include: retail fitouts and shopping centres, branding, hospitality, entertainment, commercial, corporate work and residential homes.

www.gascoigne.co.nz

Studio Guilherme Torres / p.024-027

Guilherme Torres can be defined by Daft Punk's music: work it harder, better, faster, make it over. The sentence has become his motto and it has been tattooed on his arm and written on the walls of his studio. His professional career started very early. When he was still a teenager, he worked as a designer in an engineering office, where he acquired the knowledge in the area and also the technical language. A world citizen, Guilherme divides his time between his studios in São Paulo and Londrina, with a wide range of activities, from residential and commercial projects to furniture design, one of his passions. Owner of his own and authorial style, his works were granted many awards and publications.

www.guilhermetorres.com

k&k architects / p.184-187

K&k architects was established in 2000 by Katerina Kotzia and Korina Filoxenidou. The studio deals with a variety of projects that range from exhibition design and commercial spaces to private residential projects. Projects also include participations in competitions and research programmes on urban strategies and the integration of architecture and landscape. The studio focuses on the creation of spaces that combine a strong and clear identity with an experiential nature that encourages interaction and involvement. Works often incorporate graphic, motion and lighting design, in collaboration with exceptional designers from those fields. Projects have been published in architectural magazines and catalogues.

www.kkarchitects.gr

Keiichi Hayashi Architect / p.178-179

Keiichi Hayashi was born in Osaka, Japan, 1967. Graduated from Metal Engineering, Kansai University in 1991 and Architecture, Kansai Univercity in 1993. He established Keiichi Hayashi Architect in 1997.

www.haya-at.com

KEISUKE FUJIWARA DESIGN OFFICE / p.164-167

Keisuke Fujiwara was born in 1968 in Tokyo, Japan. He graduated from the Musashino Art University, and followed to work under the renowned interior designer, Shigeru Uchida. After interning at Ron Arad Associates in 2001, he established Keisuke Fujiwara Design Office which specializes in interior and furniture design. He has been designing shops for PLEASE ISSEY MIYAKE around the world (Japan, France, China, South Korea, Taiwan and Thailand). Since establishing Keisuke Fujiwara Design Office, his works have been exhibited in the Milan furniture fair, DESIGN MIAMI and INTERIEUR in Kortrijik.

He was awarded his first prize from the Japanese Commercial Environment Designer Association. He currently holds an Associate Professor position at the Tokyo Metropolitan University.

www.keisukefujiwara.com

Kengo Kuma & Associates / *p.*044-047

Kengo Kuma won the Energy Performance + Architecture Award (France) in 2008, Decoration Officier de L'Ordre des Arts et des Lettres (France) in 2009, Mainichi Art Award for "Nezu Museum" in 2010, and the Minister of Education, Culture, Sports, Science and Technology's Art Encouragement Prize for "Yusuhara Wooden Bridge Museum" in 2011.

For Associates, Detail Prize 2007 special prize for "Chokkura Plaza and Shelter" (Germany) in 2007, Emirates Leaf Award for Public Building for Suntory Museum of Art (UK/UAE) and Design For Asia Award for "Fujiya Ryokan" (Hong Kong) in 2008, and Conde Nast Traveler Magazine's World Best New Hotels 2009 for "The Opposite House" (USA) in 2009.

www.kkaa.co.jp

Klab Architecture, Konstantinos Labrinopoulos / *p.*168-171

Klab Architecture (kinetic lab of architecture) was established at the end of 2007 by Konstantinos Labrinopoulos, the co-founder of klmf architects.

Konstantinos Labrinopoulos with a team of high talented architects from around the world is pursuing through research, high quality architectural design in any project.

With more experience and even more enthusiasm, klab aims to deliver a new architectural proposal.

Klab Architecture was featured among the 20 hottest young architecture firms in the world in the August issue and it was on the Wallpaper's Architects directory for the top 50 up and coming architectural firms in the world.

www.klab.gr

kotaro horiuchi architecture / *p.*010-031

Kotaro HORIUCHI established his own firm, kotaro horiuchi architecture in Tokyo, Nagoya and Paris in 2009. After gaining experience through world renowned architecture firms such as: DPA - Dominique Perrault Architecture (France), Mecanoo Architecten (The Netherlands), and PPAG - Popelka Poduschka Architekten (Austria), he manages offices in Tokyo, Nagoya, and Paris. As an up-coming young new generation architect. Kotaro HORIUCHI works on multiple projects around the world. His projects include both new construction and renovations of residential, retails, offices, public housings, hotel, and spas.

www. kotarohoriuchi.com

LEONG LEONG / *p.*114-119, *p.*172-177

LEONG LEONG (LLA) is a New York-based design office practicing in the fields of architecture, culture and urbanism. LLA's internationally recognized work is driven by a commitment to ideas and their realization. LLA believes the practice of architecture is a collective intelligence in constant dialogue with other disciplines, cultures, thinkers, and makers to offer new possibilities to engage the city. As a result, ideas are not generated in a vacuum but emerge from critical conversation, analysis, and experimentation. This concept-based approach to design is coupled with a deep interest in methods of production that challenge norms and reveal new territories. LLA was founded by brothers, Christopher and Dominic Leong in 2008. LLA is currently working on projects in Seoul, New York, and Napa Valley, California.

www.leong-leong.com

LOLA, Local Office for Large Architecture / *p.*148-153

LOLA is a platform focused on multi-disciplinary architecture and contemporary design. It expresses itself through the production of spaces with a responsible approach to mass and life issues, the nature of places and their materiality as a form of organized and spontaneous expression.

Collaboration and ongoing dialogue with studios and professionals from different areas enables LOLA to create a flexible and diverse background.

LOLA lays the foundations of critical, positive and pluralist thinking, followed by the development of projects in various sectors, from design to the interior, from the conversion and renovation of buildings to retail design in Spain, Italy, Portugal, Saudi Arabia, Brazil, and USA.

www.lola-architecture.com

March Studio / *p.*062-065

At March Studio, our passion is for the spaces we encounter every say – homes, businesses and public domains. We design and build the new through our architectural practice. Transform and invigorate the existing with graphic and interior design and employ our art in public spaces to inspire and surprise. Inespective of a project's scale. Our work is invanably informed by the breadth of skills and experience that reside at March Studio.

www. marchstudio.com.au

Nendo / *p.088-091, p.132-133, p.158-163, p.188-191*

Nendo was born in Toronto, Canada, 1977. M.A. in Architecture, Waseda University, Tokyo and Established "nendo" Tokyo office in 2002. Established "nendo" Milan office in 2005. Lecturer for Showa Women's University. Tokyo and "The 100 Most Respected Japanese" (Newsweek magazine) in 2006. Published "nendo" (daab) in 2008. Lecturer for Kuwasawa Design School, Tokyo in 2009. Published "nendo ghost stories" (Art Design Publishing) and won A jury member of iF award in 2010, and published "kaminendo" (Art Design Publishing) in 2011.

www.nendo.jp

O.F.D.A architects studio / *p.214-217*

Taku Sakaushi of O.F.D.A finished education as Ministry Exchange Student in UCLA, USA in 1985, and was the master of Tokyo Institute of Technology in 1986. Associate Founder of O.F.D.A.associates in 1998, and also the Professor of Tokyo University of Science.

He won "Yoshinobu Ashiwara Awards 2006" to "Re-tem Tokyo Factory" in 2005. International Architecture Award 2007 to "Re-tem Tokyo Factory" in 2007. And International Architecture Award 2010 to "Re-tem China Factory" in 2010.

www.ofda.jp

PANORAMA / *p.082-087*

The company receives a number of recognitions and awards over the years including US's IDA Design Awards, JCD Design Awards Best 100, FRAME Great Indoors Awards Nominee, iF Design Awards China, China's Most Successful Design Awards, The Ring - iC@ward International Interior Design, Asia Pacific Interior Design Awards, Hong Kong Ten Outstanding Designers Award, Hong Kong Designers Association Awards, Perspective Design Recognition Awards and Design for Asia Awards Finalist. Projects have been featured in numerous international design magazines & journals, e.g. Netherland's FRAME, Japan's World Hyper Interiors, Singapore's ISH & d+a, Korea's Interior World & bob.

www.panoramahk.com

Paradox Studio / *p.206-209*

Paradox STUDIO is a Taipei-based interior design consultancy, we are happy to work on projects of any size from major redevelopments to an individual room, from construction work to final decoration. We will handle every aspect of the job including providing you with design concepts and proposed plans.

We design of bespoke cabinetry and unique pieces of furniture, detailed construction drawings, specifications and scope of works for contractors. We are happy to work on a design and build basis with our team of contractors, to undertake a full tender procedure. We can also provide small-scale architectural solution such as individual extension and conservatories. We handle planning applications, listed building consents, party wall agreements, structural changes and any building regulations submission.

www.paradox-studio.com

ra / *p.138-141*

Ra antwerp is based on a platform for your artist, designers and artists are presented and defended within the ra structure that gather music, art, fashion, danse and others.

Ra is constantly folowing arond the world new talents to present them in the ra spaces.

Ra is an initiative by romain brau (artistic director) and anna kushnerova (director), passionately supported by a multi-talented, multi-cultural and multi-generational team

www.ra13.be

Roberto Murgia Architetto, Studio Fase, Aliverti Samsa Architetti / *p.048-051*

Born in Cagliari in 1972, he graduated in architecture in Genoa. In 1997, he moved to Milan where he collaborated with various studios, including Stefano Boeri and piuarch. studioFASE opened in 2002 with Luca Bucci, an interdisciplinary study that deals with architecture and urban planning, which develops projects at various scales. StudioFASE left in 2010 to focus on architecture, interiors and design. From 2005 deals with muji stores in Italy and, since 2009, also in France.

www.robertomurgia.it

SAKO Architects / p.032-035, p.054-057, p.102-103, p.180-183

SAKO Architects is a Beijing based architecture firm of Japanese architect Keiichiro Sako. So far, SAKO Architects has produced over 70 projects in China, Japan, Korea, Mongolia and Spain. In addition to the core services of architectural design and interior design, we also provide graphic design, furniture and urban master planning. Nowadays, we continue to develop the architecture known as, "CHINESE BRAND ARCHITECTS", using specific themes which can only be found in China.

www.sako.co.jp

Saucier + Perrotte architectes / p.092-101

The Montréal architectural firm of Saucier + Perrotte architectes was established in 1988 by Gilles Saucier and André Perrotte. Both partners graduated from the School of Architecture at Université Laval in 1982. The firm quickly placed itself at the forefront of a new generation of Québec architects, working with bold concepts, elegant planning, a keen attention to geography and climate, and precise construction details. They compose views, landscaping, and materials to make sophisticated connections between inside rooms and outside surroundings, and have an established reputation for dramatically transforming existing structures.

www.saucierperrotte.com

sinato Inc. / p.218-223

Sinato Inc. established by Chikara Ohno in 2004, and received various domestic and international awards as follows.

It won IIDA Global Excellence Awards, Honorable Mention, The Ring iC@ward international design 2010, Gold Award, Contractworld.award, New Generation Short-listed, Design For Asia, Bronze Award, Good Design Award, JCD Design Award, Gold Award, SDA Awards, Grand Prix, Display Design Award, Encouragement Prize, NDF Awards, Encouragement Prize, Best Store Of The Year, Excellent Prize, Mie Architecture Awards, Gunma Agricultural Technology Center Design Competition, Honorable Mention, TOTO Remodel Style Contest, Grand Prix, NASHOP Lighting Awards, Excellent Prize, and more.

www.sinato.jp

Snarkitecture / p.120-123

Snarkitecture is a collaborative practice operating in territories between the disciplines of art and architecture. Working within existing spaces or in collaboration with other artists and designers, the practice focuses on the investigation of structure, material and program and how these elements can be manipulated to serve new and imaginative purposes. Searching for sites within architecture with the possibility for confusion or misuse, Snarkitecture aims to make architecture perform the unexpected. Snarkitecture was established by Daniel Arsham and Alex Mustonen.

www.snarkitecture.com

SHIMOKAWA Toru / p.144-147, p.204-205

Born in Fukuoka Japan 1983. Studied Architecture by himself, then established "stad" in 2005. His First Architecture called S-house completed in 2007 was awarded Bauwelt Prize 2009 in Berlin, and chosen one of The World's 30 Architect of Wallpaper* Architects Directory 2009. And was Invited to exhibit of International Architecture Biennale Rotterdam 2009 in Chabot Museum, Rotterdam.

www.65x45.com

Toby Horrocks Architecture and Autumn Products / p.052-053

Toby Horrocks is an architect that started designing cardboard furniture after moving into an empty rental apartment. As well as Freefold Furniture, he runs his own architecture practice, Toby Horrocks Architecture in Melbourne. Kristian Aus is an industrial designer that has worked in design consultancies across all areas of product design. He runs Autumn Products, a small, Sydney based design consultancy that aims to produce work that is fun and provokes a smile. This is their first collaboration.

www.tobyhorrocks.com

Tokujin Yoshioka Inc. / p.078-081, p.110-113

Born in Saga, Japan in 1967. Worked under Shiro Kuramata in 1987 and Issey Miyake since 1988 and established his own studio, Tokujin Yoshioka Design in 2000.

He has done many projects with Issey Miyake for nearly 20 years such as shop design and installation for A-POC and ISSEY MIYAKE. Also, he has collaborated with various companies in and outside Japan such as HERMES, TOYOTA, BMW, KDDI, SWAROVSKI, and other noted ones.

www.tokujin.com

Tomás Alonso Design Studio / p.124-127

Born in Vigo, Spain, Tomás Alonso has been travelling since the age of 19 to pursue his career as a designer. He has been living, studying and working in the USA, Italy and Australia before moving to London to complete a MA at the Royal College of Art.

He combines his research and commercial design work with occasional teaching of workshops; most recently he has taught a few workshops at ÉCAL in Lausanne, Switzerland.

www.tomas-alonso.com

TORAFU ARCHITECTS / p.104-109, p.192-203

Founded in 2004 by Koichi Suzuno and Shinya Kamuro. TORAFU ARCHITECTS employs a working approach based on architectural thinking. Works by the duo include a diverse range of products. From architectural design to interior design for shops, exhibition space design, product design. Spatial installations and film making. They have received many prizes including the Design for Asia (DFA)Grand Award for the "TEMPLATE IN CLASKA" in 2005, and the Grand Prize of the Elita Design Awards 2011 with "Light Loom Salone 2011". The "airvase book" and "TORAFU ARCHITECTS Ideas + Process 2004-2011" were published in 2011.

www. torafu.com

VAÍLLO & IRIGARAY + GALAR / p.074-077

VAILLO+IRIGARAY ARCHITECTS confers on its projects a vitally important nuance: multifocality.

Multifocality consists on a polyhedric view of the project, so that it offers solutions to every raised problem, and sets up a functional hierarchy as well as a wide capacity for shape synthesis. Constant collaboration with every agent of the complex process provides a global vision and the appropriate solution, that is also enhanced by different outlooks.

Only from the very definite is feasible to offer universal solutions. It is thus that our working method consists of the resolution of the problems raised by the project itself. The work material is, as it has been explained, the prime mover, the basis, the project concept and the essential raw material.

www.vailloirigaray.com

WE Architecture / p.014-017

WE Architecture, founded in 2008, is a young innovating architecture office, based in Copenhagen, Denmark. Our capability spans from architecture, urban strategies, tangible design and utopian ideas.

WE believes that the best result emerge through teamwork and transdisciplinary networks. That is why WE Architecture work across continents as well as across professional borders to enter complex conditions with the best insight and precision.

We create proposals that merge through creative translation of all the information we all get from contexts, conditions and programs.

WE Architecture strive to push innovative architecture forward to improve the condition of the world. No less.

www.we-a.dk

ZMIK in collaboration with SÜDQUAI patente.unikate. / p.070-073

ZMIK is a spacial design studio with a focus on creating identity, individuality and communication in space. ZMIK exists to create unique, bold and accurate spacial environments. ZMIK operates at the fringes of various disciplines, such as interior design, scenography, architecture, object design and installation, blending these to achieve integrated solutions to complex questions.

ZMIK was founded by Rolf Indermühle, Mattias Mohr and Magnus Zwyssig in Basel/Switzerland in 2006. ZMIK works on projects in different scales starting from singular objects in space over interiors up to architectonical transformations. Our clients include, amongst others, Art Basel, Belux, Engadiner Museum St. Moritz, Swiss Architecture Museum, Swiss Federal Office of Culture and UBS Fund Management.

www.zmik.ch

ACKNOWLEDGEMENTS

We would like to thank all the architects and designers for their kind permission to publish their works, as well as all the photographers who have generously granted us the rights to use their images. We are also very grateful to many other people whose names do not appear on the credits but who made specific contributions and provided support. Without them, we would not be able to share these beautiful commercial spaces with readers around the world.